The
Garland Library
of
War and Peace

The
Garland Library
of
War and Peace

Under the General Editorship of
Blanche Wiesen Cook, *John Jay College, C.U.N.Y.*
Sandi E. Cooper, *Richmond College, C.U.N.Y.*
Charles Chatfield, *Wittenberg University*

The First American Peace Movement

comprising

War Inconsistent with the Religion of Jesus Christ

by

David Low Dodge

with an introduction by

Edwin D. Mead

The Lawfulness of War for Christians, Examined

by

James Mott

A Solemn Review of the Custom of War

by

Noah Worcester

with a new introduction
for the Garland Edition by

Peter Brock

Garland Publishing, Inc., New York & London
1972

Library of Congress Cataloging in Publication Data
Main entry under title:

The First American peace movement.

(The Garland library of war and peace)
    Reprint of three works originally published in 1905,
1814, and 1815, respectively.
    1. Peace--Addresses, essays, lectures. 2. War--
Addresses, essays, lectures. I. Dodge, David Low,
1774-1852. War inconsistent with the religion of
Jesus Christ. 1972. II. Mott, James, 1743-1823.
The lawfulness of war for Christians, examined. 1972.
III. Worcester, Noah, 1758-1837. A solemn review of
the custom of war. 1972. IV. Series.
JX1949.F57 1972   261.8'73   73-147428
ISBN 0-8240-0220-2

Introduction

The antiwar demonstrators who in the late 1960's and early 1970's have filled the streets of Washington and other major cities in the United States, the draft-card burners and conscientious objectors to military service, have probably been, for the most part, oblivious of the deep roots which antimilitarism has had in the American tradition. And, it would seem, their "hawkish" antagonists have remained equally unaware of this fact — at least if we may judge by their many statements implying that antimilitarism is in some way an un-American activity.

I do not know when the first case of an American conscientious objection to military service occurred. Possibly, it may have been as early as 1627. The manuscript Decisions of the Virginia General Court *contain an entry dated May 7 of that year, recording the complaint of a militia officer that one "Richard Buckley hath resisted and opposed him, in his command, in denying to take arms and discharge his public duty." And the minute concludes: "The Court hath ordered, that for this offence he shall be laid neck and heels 12 hours, and at the crop by way of fine shall pay 100 lbs. of tobacco." Buckley, then, was certainly an objector. Unfortunately, the court minute does not tell us enough to determine whether*

5

he was indeed a conscientious *objector. Perhaps he refused to take up arms and discharge his duties in the local militia because he was lazy or just disliked authority, rather than because he entertained genuine scruples against killing his fellow men. We do not know. I am, however, on safe ground if I date the beginnings of American pacifism to the 1650's and the coming of the first Quakers to this continent.*

The Quakers — or Society of Friends, as this religious sect came to be known — had originated around 1650 in Oliver Cromwell's England. Their founder was an ex-cobbler and man of the people, George Fox. Quakers eventually settled in all the American colonies from Georgia to Maine; at the beginning, in some areas (for example Pennsylvania) for a time they even formed a majority of the population. The Quakers were religious pacifists, for they held that war and violence were contrary to the Inner Light of Christ's spirit, which, they believed, shines within all men. The influence on the American peace movement of Quaker pacifism has been great (Friend Richard Nixon notwithstanding!). Indeed, until the present century so close was the identification in the popular mind of Quakerism with pacifism that a non-Quaker pacifist would often in explanation of his position say simply: "I hold Quaker views on war."

In the seventeenth and eighteenth centuries American Quakers often got into trouble with the law because of their refusal to drill with the militia, an obligation encumbent on all ablebodied males, except in Pennsylvania while it was under Quaker control (1682-1756). Quakers at that period were all what we would call today absolutist objectors, that is, they demanded unconditional exemption from service when called upon for the militia and refused any alternative offered by the authorities in lieu of military service. For Quakers considered that the state had no right to demand either alternative civilian service or payment of a fine (this last was the usual way-out offered to Quaker conscientious objectors) from a man who was only acting according to the dictates of his conscience. Quaker objectors, therefore, suffered distraint, i.e., confiscation, of their property as punishment for their behavior; when they possessed no property to distrain, they were put in prison. However, usually neither distraints nor imprisonment were in actual fact excessively burdensome. Those Quakers who did not conform to the rules of their church and either did their military service or paid their militia fines were "disowned", i.e., expelled from their church. It was not until the mid-nineteenth century that the Quakers relaxed their church discipline, allowing differences of opinion to exist on war and a host of other social and moral issues.

There was indeed something narrow and constricting about the pacifism of the early Quakers, alongside great sincerity and depth of religious belief. These Quaker pacifists exhibited admirable devotion

7

INTRODUCTION

*to principle and witnessed to the desirability of peace
in a world in which the glamor of war held almost
uncontested sway over men's minds. But the sectarian
character of this witness prevented them from mount-
ing any wider peace movement which would embrace
men and women of other faiths and different ways of
thought.*

*In the course of time Quakers produced an
extensive expository literature in connection with
their peace testimony. A representative example of
this literature as it had developed by the early
nineteenth century is the pamphlet by the Quaker
merchant and philanthropist, James Mott, Senior
(1742-1823), reprinted in this volume. Mott, we
should note, employs not only the traditional Quaker
arguments against war founded strictly on religious
faith but also the more secular antimilitarist reasoning
of the Christian humanist Erasmus.*

*Before the nineteenth century the pacifist and
antiwar position had been almost entirely confined to
the peace sects: Quakers as well as such denomina-
tions as the Mennonites and Dunkers, who are also
still to be found in the United States today. Outside
such groups an isolated individual, it is true, would
occasionally raise his voice in protest against war. But
it is not really until the beginning of the nineteenth
century that we discover pacifistic stirrings among
sections of the population unconnected with the
peace sects. From then onward, a growing number,
particularly among the clergy, though still only a*

handful in comparison with the war-approving majority, began to attack the institution *of war — "the custom of war", as the phrase went — both on humanitarian as well as on Christian grounds. And to this censure of war on moral grounds came in 1812, after the outbreak of hostilities between the United States and Great Britain, a wave of political and economic antimilitarism throughout the New England states. Peace came in 1815. But the crusade against war continued.*

"Crusade against war": this is the apt phrase used by Merle E. Curti for the title of his pioneering study of the antebellum peace movement, first published in 1929. The peace advocates of that period shared the quasi-religious enthusiasm and the messianic zeal of the contemporary crusaders in such causes as anti-slavery, temperance, penal reform, women's rights, etc.. Indeed, all these causes, pacifism along with the rest, formed part of an all-embracing movement of humanitarian reform, and often the membership lists of the various reform societies largely overlapped.

"The world in 1815 had particular reason to be weary of war", writes Curti. It is no coincidence, then, that the world's first peace societies sprang up at that date within a few months of each other, yet quite independently. The first in point of time was the New York Peace Society, started in 1815 by a Presbyterian layman, the well-to-do city merchant David Low Dodge (1774-1852). It was followed in quick succession by other peace societies, in Massa-

chusetts and Ohio in the same year and in London in 1816. Of the American societies the Massachusetts Peace Society was the most important; it still exists today under the name American Peace Society, though no longer particularly active. Its founder was an amiable Unitarian clergyman, the Rev. Noah Worcester (1758-1837).

The two peace tracts which Dodge and Worcester published at the conclusion of the Napoleonic wars (they are both reprinted in this volume along with Dodge's earlier pamphlet The Mediator's Kingdom *which he brought out in 1809) soon became classics of the peace movement, and successive generations of peace workers on both sides of the Atlantic drew strength from these writings. Influenced to some extent by the ideas of the eighteenth-century Enlightenment, Dodge and Worcester made use of the utilitarian case against war alongside religious arguments (though neither they nor other early nineteenth-century advocates of peace penetrated very deeply into the economic causes of conflict). They were divided, however, concerning the limits of pacifism. Whereas Worcester in his* Solemn Review *did not explicitly condemn "defensive" war but strove rather to create an enlightened public opinion, which would make all war impossible between civilized nations, Dodge in his writings on peace took the uncompromising Quaker view that all wars, including wars of defense, were incompatible with the Christian religion. Whereas Dodge looked askance at any who*

INTRODUCTION

fell short of the complete pacifist position, Worcester welcomed into his Massachusetts Peace Society all who sincerely wished to work for a peaceable world. "We intend", he wrote, "that this society shall be established on principles so broad, as to embrace the friends of peace who differ on this as on other subjects." This dichotomy between absolute pacifists and moderate pacificists, which we find exemplified in the case of Dodge and Worcester, has continued down to the present day. Thus, in their differences as in their similarities, the two men typify some of the basic attitudes found in the modern peace movement.

Peter Brock
Department of History
University of Toronto

DAVID LOW DODGE

WAR INCONSISTENT

WITH THE

RELIGION OF JESUS CHRIST

BY

DAVID LOW DODGE

WITH AN INTRODUCTION

BY

EDWIN D. MEAD

———•◦•———

PUBLISHED FOR THE INTERNATIONAL UNION
GINN & COMPANY, BOSTON
1905

CONTENTS

                                         PAGE

INTRODUCTION vii

WAR INCONSISTENT WITH THE RELIGION OF JESUS CHRIST   I

WAR IS INHUMAN:

    I. Because it hardens the heart and blunts the tender
       feelings of mankind 2

   II. War is inhuman, as in its nature and tendency it
       abuses God's animal creation 6

  III. War is inhuman, as it oppresses the poor 8

  IV. War is inhuman, as it spreads terror and distress
       among mankind 12

   V. War is inhuman, as it involves men in fatigue, famine,
       and all the pains of mutilated bodies 14

  VI. War is inhuman, as it destroys the youth and cuts
       off the hope of gray hairs 16

 VII. War is inhuman, as it multiplies widows and orphans,
       and clothes the land in mourning 18

WAR IS UNWISE:

    I. Because, instead of preventing, it provokes insult
       and mischief 23

   II. War is unwise, for instead of diminishing, it increases
       difficulties 26

  III. War is unwise, because it destroys property 28

  IV. War is unwise, as it is dangerous to the liberties of
       men 30

   V. War is unwise, as it diminishes the happiness of
       mankind 34

  VI. War is unwise, as it does not mend, but injures, the
       morals of society 36

PAGE

VII. War is unwise, as it is hazarding eternal things for
only the chance of defending temporal things . 42

VIII. War is unwise, as it does not answer the professed
end for which it is intended 44

WAR IS CRIMINAL :

I. Going to war is not keeping from the appearance
of evil, but is running into temptation 47

II. War is criminal, as it naturally inflames the pride
of man 49

III. War necessarily infringes on the consciences of
men, and therefore is criminal 52

IV. War is criminal, as it is opposed to patient suffering
under unjust and cruel treatment 56

V. War is criminal, as it is not doing to others as we
should wish them to do to us 60

VI. War is inconsistent with mercy, and is therefore
criminal 61

VII. War is criminal, as the practice of it is inconsistent
with forgiving trespasses as we wish to be forgiven
by the final judge 63

VIII. Engaging in war is not manifesting love to enemies
or returning good for evil 64

IX. War is criminal, because it is actually rendering
evil for evil 67

X. War is criminal, as it is actually doing evil that good
may come ; and this is the best apology that can
be made for it 71

XI. War is opposed to the example of the Son of God,
and is therefore criminal 72

OBJECTIONS ANSWERED 77

HYMN 121

THE MEDIATOR'S KINGDOM NOT OF THIS WORLD : BUT
SPIRITUAL 123

INTRODUCTION

To David Low Dodge of New York belongs the high honor of having written the first pamphlets published in America directed expressly against the war system of nations, and of having founded the first peace society ever organized in America or in the world. His first pamphlet, *The Mediator's Kingdom not of this World*, was published in 1809. His second and more important pamphlet, *War Inconsistent with the Religion of Jesus Christ*, was prepared for the press in 1812. This was two years before the publication of Noah Worcester's *Solemn Review of the Custom of War*, which was issued in Boston on Christmas Day, 1814. Early in 1812 Mr. Dodge and his friends in New York deliberated on the expediency of forming a peace society; but on account of the excitement attending the war with Great Britain this was postponed until 1815. In August of that year the New York Peace Society, the first in the world, was organized, with Mr. Dodge as its president. This was four months before the organization of the Massachusetts Peace Society (December 26, 1815) under the leadership of Noah Worcester, and nearly a year before the English Peace Society, the first in Europe, was formed (June 14, 1816) in London.

The preëminent historical interest attaching to Mr. Dodge's pioneering work in the peace cause in this country would alone justify and indeed seem to command

the republication of his pamphlets at this time, when
the great ideas for which he so courageously and pro-
phetically stood are at last winning the general recog-
nition of humane and thoughtful men. But it is not
merely historical interest which warrants a revival of
attention to these almost forgotten papers. Their intrin-
sic power and worth are such as make their reading,
especially that of the second essay, *War Inconsistent
with the Religion of Jesus Christ*, which stands first
in the present volume, edifying and inspiring to-day.
Marked by few literary graces and cast in a theological
mold which the critical thought of the present has in
large measure outgrown, there is a force of thought, a
moral earnestness, a persevering logic, a common sense,
a hatred of inhumanity, a passion for justice, a penetra-
tion and a virtue in them, which commends them to the
abiding and reverent regard of all who work for the
peace and order of the world. Among such workers
to-day are men of various political philosophies, and
perhaps only a small minority are nonresistants of the
extreme type of David L. Dodge; but to that minority,
we cannot fail to remark, belongs the greatest and most
influential of all the peace prophets of this time, Leo
Tolstoi. None can read these old essays without being
impressed by the fact that their arguments are essen-
tially the same as those of the great Russian. There is
little indeed of the Tolstoian thunder and lightning, the
pathos, wrath, and rhetoric, the poetry and prophecy, in
these old-fashioned pages; but the doctrine is the same
as that of *Bethink Yourselves!* and *Patriotism versus
Christianity*. In his central thought and purpose, in his

religious trust and reliance upon the Christian principle, the New York merchant was a Tolstoi a hundred years before his time.

David Low Dodge was born June 14, 1774, in that part of Pomfret, Connecticut, now called Brooklyn. This was the home of Israel Putnam ; and David Dodge's father, a farmer and carpenter, was Putnam's neighbor and friend, — may well have been near him when in April, 1775, upon hearing of the battle of Lexington, he left his plow in the furrow and started to join the forces gathering at Cambridge. David Dodge's father, grandfather, and great-grandfather each bore the name of David Dodge. The great-grandfather was a Congregational minister, who was understood to have come from Wales, — a learned and wealthy man, who was for a while settled in the vicinity of Cape Ann in Massachusetts. The grandfather, who also received a liberal education, probably in England, came into the possession of his father's estate, for that day a large one, and we are not informed whether he followed any profession or regular business. He was a man fully six feet tall, of great muscular power, and a lover of good horses, on which he spent much time and money. He married Ann Low, from a wealthy Massachusetts family, and settled in Beverly, where their sons David and Samuel were born, and where the family fortunes became much embarrassed. About 1757 the family removed to Pomfret, Connecticut, and the boys, whose education at the hands of their mother had been but slight, were apprenticed, David to a carpenter and Samuel to a shoemaker. Their father, obtaining at this time a commission in the army invading Canada, met his death in a bateau which attempted to descend the falls of the Oswego and was dashed to pieces on the rocks with the loss of every soul on board.

David Low Dodge's mother, when a girl, was Mary Stuart, and when she married his father, in 1768, was a widow bearing the name of Earl. The young husband hired a small farm, the wife by her industry and economy had furniture sufficient to begin housekeeping, and the little home was founded in which David Low Dodge's only sister Mary was born in 1770. Three years later the father hired a more expensive place in the same town, where the boy was born in 1774. "During that year," he writes in his autobiography, "my father became serious, and commenced family prayer. He was educated in the old semi-Arminian views of his mother and the halfway covenant. My mother was a rigid Calvinist of the Whitefield school. Neither of them ever made a public profession of religion, but they were careful to observe external ordinances, catechize their children, and give religious instruction. They were honest, industrious, temperate, kind-hearted people, universally respected and esteemed by all who were acquainted with them."

Such was the atmosphere in which the boy grew up. "The American Revolution at this period was convulsing the whole country, drafting and enlisting soldiers. Wagons were needed for the army, and by the advice of the Putnams, the old general and his son Israel, who was about two years younger than my father, he was induced to engage in the manufacture of continental wagons. He hired a convenient place for carpenters and blacksmiths,

took several journeymen into the family, and embarked
all his earnings in the business." The boy's half-brothers,
William and Jesse Earl, entered the army at the tender
ages of fourteen and sixteen, endured battles, sickness,
and every privation, and both died towards the close of
the war, the event almost wrecking the nervous system
of the mother, a woman of acute sensibility. Thus early
were the horrors of war brought personally home to the
boy. He remembered hearing the distant cannonading
when New London was burned by the British, and the
exclamation of the man beside him, "Blood is flowing
to-day." "News came the next morning that the forts
were stormed, the garrisons put to the sword, New London burnt, and the British were marching upon Norwich,
and would proceed up into the country. My mother
wrung her hands, and asked my father if we had not
better pack up some things to secrete them."

The boy's education was slight and fragmentary.
The summer he was six years old he attended the
school of a venerable Irish maiden lady about sixty years
of age, learning Watts' *Divine Songs*, texts of Scripture,
and the *Shorter Catechism*. From the age of seven to
fourteen — the family now living on a farm in the neighboring town of Hampton — he attended the district
school for two terms each winter, having no access to
any other books than the primer, spelling book, arithmetic, and Bible. "I used often, when not at work in
the shop evenings, to retire to the old kitchen fireplace,
put my lamp into the oven, and, sitting with my back
against it, take my arithmetic, slate, and pencil, and try
to cipher a little. I often think how I should have been

delighted to have had one fifth part of the advantages enjoyed by most of my descendants." Confined to the house for seven weeks a little later as the result of accidents, he turned hungrily to such books as he could secure — Dilworth's *Arithmetic*, Webster's *Abridged Grammar*, and Salmon's *Universal English Geography*. " This opened a new and astonishing field to me for contemplation. I now obtained the first glimpse of the boundaries of land and water, of the lofty mountains, and of the mighty rivers which had cut their channels through the earth. I read and surveyed the maps and meditated upon them until I began to lecture to my young companions, and was considered quite learned in geography. Having an object in view, I began to thirst for knowledge, and succeeded in borrowing in succession *The Travels of Cyrus, Xerxes' Expedition into Greece, The History of Alexander the Great*, and *Hannibal's Invasion of Rome*." He proposed and brought about the formation of a society of young men in the town, for the improvement of minds and manners. There were fourteen young men, with an equal number of young women presently added, each furnishing a useful book as the beginning of a library. " We obtained some of the British classics, such as the *Spectator, Guardian*, etc., with a few histories ; the subjects formed a foundation for conversation when we met together."

Now the young man's ambition turned from farming to school-teaching. He began with district schools, becoming a successful teacher from the start, prosecuting his own studies assiduously in every leisure hour, fired with a desire to improve the schools, which were everywhere as wretched as can well be imagined. For some months in 1795 he left teaching to join other young men in building a bridge at Tiverton, Rhode Island. Then he attended the academy at North Canterbury, Connecticut, under the charge of the eminent teacher, John Adams. " This was the only opportunity I ever enjoyed of attending a good school, and this was abridged to fulfill my engagement to teach the town school in Mansfield." In 1796 he opened a private school in Norwich, adding the next year a morning school for young ladies and an evening school for apprentices and clerks, all of which flourished. During this time he was profoundly interested in religious matters, attending many revivals and becoming more and more concerned with moral and social problems. Now, too, he married, his wife being a daughter of Aaron Cleveland of Norwich, a strong character, afterwards a clergyman, " whose name you will find enrolled among the poets of Connecticut," and who as early as 1775 published a poem on slavery, which, condemning slavery as wholly antichristian, attracted a good deal of notice. He was the first man in Connecticut to arraign slavery publicly. Elected to the General Assembly from Norwich on that issue, he introduced a bill in behalf of emancipation.

With health somewhat impaired and with family cares increasing, David Dodge now turned from teaching to trade. First it was as a clerk in Norwich, then as a partner in a general store, then as head of various dry goods establishments in Hartford and other Connecticut towns, always and everywhere successful. In 1805 Messrs. S. and H. Higginson of Boston, cousins of his wife, a firm of high standing and large capital, made him a proposition to enter into a copartnership with a view to establishing an extensive importing and jobbing store in the city of New York ; and he accepted the proposition, going to New York the next year to take charge of the concern in that city. He took a store in Pearl Street, and the year afterwards the family took possession of the house connected with the store, still reserving the house in Hartford as a retreat in case of yellow fever in New York. From this time until his death, April 23, 1852, New York was, with occasional interruptions, his home and the center of his varied and ever enlarging activities. Just before the outbreak of the war with England his partners became bankrupt through losses in extensive shipping of American produce to Europe. "Bonaparte sprung his trap upon more than a million dollars of their property." Mr. Dodge now established cotton factories in Connecticut, and later commenced anew the dry goods business in New York, his home for years alternating between New York and the Norwich neighborhood ; and for the nine years following 1835 he occupied a large farm in Plainfield, New Jersey.

Active as was his business life, and faithful his devotion to his large business affairs, — and he came to rank with the most prominent mercantile men of his day, — his mind was always intent upon social and religious subjects. "During the years of 1808 to 1811 our business became extensive and demanded much thought and attention ; yet I think my affections were on the subject of religion." Revivals of religion, the interests of his church in Norwich or New York, the improvement of the lives of his factory operatives, the organization in New York of the Christian Friendly Society for the Promotion of Morals and Religion, — such were the objects which commanded him. Throughout his long residence in New York he was a prominent worker in the Presbyterian church, for many years an elder in the church. He took a leading part in organizing the New York Bible Society and the New York Tract Society, was much engaged in the early missionary movements in New York, and in promoting the education of young men for the ministry. He was a lover of knowledge, a great reader, and one who thought and wrote as he read. Deeply interested in history, ancient and modern, his chief interest was in theological discussion. He was familiar with the chief theological controversies of the day, and upon many of them committed his views to writing. His knowledge of the Bible was remarkable; he read it through critically in course forty-two times. He held firmly the Calvinistic system of doctrine, and he addressed to his children a series of letters, characterized by great ability and logical force, in defense of the faith, and constituting together a compendious system of theology.

Several of these letters are included in the memorial volume published for the family in 1854 under the editorial supervision of Rev. Matson M. Smith. This volume contains, besides the two essays on war here reprinted, and various verses and letters, the interesting autobiography which he prepared, at the request of his children, a few years before his death, and a supplementary biographical sketch by his pastor, Rev. Asa D.

Smith. In the mass of manuscripts which he left behind was an essay upon " The Relation of the Church to the World," and one upon " Retributive Judgment and Capital Punishment,"— to which he was sharply opposed. He was opposed indeed to so much in human governments as now constituted, — "whose ultimate reliance," he said, " is the sword," and whose laws he felt to be so often contrary to the laws of Christ to which he gave his sole allegiance, — that he would neither vote nor hold office. Strict and inflexible as he was in his views of political and religious duty, he was one of the most genial and delightful of men, a Christian in whom there was no guile, fond of the young, affectionate, courteous, "given to hospitality," " careful habitually to make even the conventionalities of life a fitting accompaniment and expression of the inward principle of kindness." A face as strong as it is gentle, and as gentle as it is strong, is that which looks at us in the beautiful portrait preserved in the family treasures, and a copy of which forms the frontispiece of the present volume.

The character and influence of the family which he founded in New York, during the three generations which have followed, constitute an impressive witness to David Dodge's force and worth, his religious consecration, and high public spirit. At the junction of Broadway and Sixth Avenue stands the statue of his son, William Earl Dodge, whose life of almost fourscore years ended in 1883. For long years the head of the great house of Phelps, Dodge & Co., the manager of immense railway, lumber, and mining interests, the president of the New York Chamber of Commerce, a representative

of New York in Congress, a leader in large work for
temperance, for the freedmen, for the Indians, for theological education, for a score of high patriotic and phil-
anthropic interests, New York had in his time no more
representative, more useful, or more honored citizen.
And what is said of him may be said in almost the same
words of William Earl Dodge, his son, who died but
yesterday, and who combined broad business and phil-
anthropic activities in the same strong and influential way
as his father and grandfather before him.   President of
many religious and benevolent associations, he was pre-
eminently a patriot and an international man.   The logic
of his life and of his heritage placed him naturally at
the head of the National Arbitration Committee, which
was appointed at the great conference on international
arbitration held at Washington in the spring of 1896, following the anxiety attendant upon President Cleveland's
Venezuelan message, — a committee which, under his
chairmanship, and since his death that of Hon. John
W. Foster, has during the decade rendered such great
service to the peace and arbitration cause in this country.   It is to be noted also that the names of his son and
daughter, Cleveland H. Dodge and Grace H. Dodge,
names so conspicuously associated to-day with charitable, religious, and educational efforts in New York,
are associated, too, like his with the commanding cause
of the world's peace and better organization; both names
stand upon the American Committee of the Thirteenth
International Peace Congress, which met in Boston in
1904. Thus have the generations which have followed
him well learned and strongly emphasized the lesson

taught by David Dodge almost a century ago, that war is "inhuman, unwise, and criminal," and "inconsistent with the religion of Jesus Christ."

It was in 1805 that a startling personal experience prompted the train of thought which soon and forever made David L. Dodge the advocate of the thorough-going peace principles with which his name is chiefly identified, and led him to condemn all violence, even in self-defense, in dealings between men, as between nations. Accustomed to carry pistols when traveling with large sums of money, he was almost led to shoot his landlord in a tavern at Providence, Rhode Island, who by some blunder had come into his room at night and suddenly waked him. The thought of what his situation and feelings would have been had he taken the man's life shocked him into most searching thinking. For two or three years his mind dwelt on the question. He turned to the teaching and example of Christ, and became per-suaded that these were inconsistent with violence and the carrying of deadly weapons, and with war. The common churchman sanctioned such things, but not the early Christians; and he found strong words condemn-ing war in Luther and Erasmus, the Moravians and Quakers. Discussing the matter with many pious and Christian men, he found them generally avoiding the gospel standard. He was shocked by the "general want of faith in the promises"; but he himself laid aside at once his pistols and the fear of robbers. He became absolutely convinced that fighting and warfare were "unlawful for the followers of Christ"; and from now on he began to bear public testimony against the war spirit.

Early in the spring of 1809 he published his essay, *The Mediator's Kingdom not of this World*, which attracted so much attention that in two weeks nearly a thousand copies were sold. Three literary men joined in preparing a spirited and sarcastic criticism of it; and he immediately published a rejoinder. *The Mediator's Kingdom* was republished in Philadelphia and in Providence, and Mr. Dodge writes truly: "These publications gave the first impulse in America, if we except the uniform influence of the Friends, to inquiry into the lawfulness of war by Christians. Some who were favorable to the doctrines of peace judged that, with a bold hand, I had carried the subject too far; and doubtless, as it was new and had not been much discussed, I wrote too unguardedly, not sufficiently defining my terms. The Rev. Dr. Noah Worcester was one who so judged, and a few years after he published his very spirited and able essay, *The Solemn Review of War*." This famous essay of Worcester's represents the platform of the great body of American peace workers for a century, the position of men like Channing and Ladd and Jay and Sumner; but to a nonresistant and opponent even of self-defense, like David Dodge, these seemed the exponents of a halfway covenant.

Mr. Dodge entered into private correspondence on the lawfulness of war with Rev. Lyman Beecher, Rev. Aaron Cleveland, his father-in-law, Rev. John B. Romeyn, and Rev. Walter King. He preserved among his manuscripts letters of twenty-five pages from Dr. Romeyn and Mr. Cleveland, and copies of his reply to Dr. Romeyn (one hundred and thirty-two pages) and to Dr. Beecher (forty-four pages). Important letters from Dr. Beecher and Governor Jay he had lost. All these took the position of Dr. Worcester, sanctioning strictly defensive war in extreme cases, — all except Mr. Cleveland, who finally came into complete accord with Mr. Dodge, and published two able sermons on "The Life of Man Inviolable by the Laws of Christ."

Early in 1812 the friends of peace whom Mr. Dodge had gathered about him in New York conferred upon the forming of a peace society, "wholly confined to decided evangelical Christians, with a view to diffusing peace principles in the churches, avoiding all party questions." There being at this juncture, however, intense political feeling over the threatened war with Great Britain, they feared their motives would be misapprehended, and decided for the moment simply to act individually in diffusing information. Mr. Dodge was appointed to prepare an essay on the subject of war, stating and answering objections ; and, removing at this time to Norwich, he there, in a period of great business perplexity, completed his remarkable paper on "War Inconsistent with the Christian Religion," which was published in the very midst of the war with England.

Upon his return to New York, the friends of peace there had two or three meetings relative to the organization of a society ; and in August, 1815, they formed the New York Peace Society, of between thirty and forty members, their strict articles of association condemning all war, offensive and defensive, as wholly opposed to the example and spirit and precepts of Christ. The peace societies formed immediately afterwards in Massachusetts,

Ohio, Rhode Island, and London were organized, according to Mr. Dodge, without any knowledge of each other, the movements being the simultaneous separate results of a common impulse. Of the New York society Mr. Dodge was unanimously elected president. Monthly meetings were arranged, and at the first of these Mr. Dodge read an address upon "The Kingdom of Peace under the Benign Reign of Messiah," of which a thousand copies were at once printed and circulated. Within two years the society had increased to sixty members, men active not only against war — which the society regarded as "the greatest temporal evil, as almost every immorality is generated in its prosecution, and poverty, distress, famine, and pestilence follow in its train" — but in all the benevolent enterprises of that day. "Several respectable clergymen united with the society, — Rev. Drs. E. D. Griffin and M. L. Parvine, Rev. E. W. Baldwin (to whose pen we were much indebted), Rev. Samuel Whelpley, and his son, Rev. Melancthon Whelpley, Rev. H. G. Ufford, and Rev. S. H. Cox. Dr. Cox, however, afterwards entertained different views on the subject."

The New York Peace Society had friendly correspondence with all the other peace societies, and for several years took two hundred copies of Dr. Worcester's *Friend of Peace*. This seems finally to have contributed to divide the society, some relinquishing the non-resistant views of Mr. Dodge and adopting Worcester's less extreme position. But our brave Tolstoian was a "thorough," and never wavered. "If it was morally wrong for individuals to quarrel and fight, instead of returning good for evil," — these are his last words on the subject in his autobiography, — "it was much more criminal for communities and nations to return evil for evil, and not strive to overcome evil with good. In fact, the great barrier to our progress was the example of our fathers in the American Revolution. That they were generally true patriots, in the political sense of the term, and many hopefully pious, I would not call in question, while I consider them as ill directed by education as St. Paul was when on his way to Damascus."

The New York Peace Society maintained its existence and work for many years. In 1828 it united with other societies in the creation of the American Peace Society, which was organized in New York on May 8 of that year on the initiative of William Ladd. After this the New York society seems to have done little separate work, and finally its independent existence ceased. Mr. Dodge assisted in the organization of the new national society, and presided at its first annual meeting, May 13, 1829. He was chosen a member of its board of directors, and later became a life director, maintaining his connection with the society until his death in 1852, faithful to the end to the radical views by which he had become so powerfully possessed almost half a century before.

For two generations New York has been without a local peace society. The services of eminent individual citizens of the city and state of New York for the peace cause during that period, however, have been signal. Judge William Jay of New York was for a decade president of the American Peace Society, — the important decade covering the great peace congresses in Europe at the middle of the last century; and it was his proposal that an arbitration clause should be attached to future commercial treaties which furnished the basis for the most constructive debates of the first congress, that at London in 1843. The three really important members of the American delegation at The Hague Conference were citizens of New York, — Andrew D. White, Seth Low, and Frederick W. Holls. A remarkable plan adopted by the New York State Bar Association suggested important features of The Hague Court as finally constituted. It is a citizen of New York, Andrew Carnegie, who has given $1,500,000 for a worthy building for the court at The Hague, — a temple of peace. Mr. Carnegie, whose influence in behalf of international fraternity is perhaps second to that of no other to-day, has also given $5,000,000 to establish a pension fund for "heroes of peace," whose heroism, too long comparatively neglected, he rightly sees to be not less than the heroism of the soldier. The most important series of arbitration conferences in recent times have been those at Lake Mohonk, in the state of New York, arranged by Albert K. Smiley, — conferences of growing size and importance, commanding world-wide attention, and performing for this country almost the same service performed for France and England by their national peace congresses. Finally, it must not be forgotten that Theodore Roosevelt, the President of the United States, through whose initiative the second Hague Conference will presently meet, is also a citizen of New York.

At this very time a promising movement is gaining head to organize once more in David Dodge's city a New York Peace Society. At one of the recent Mohonk

INTRODUCTION

ʾrences a large committee of New York men, under
ħe chairmanship of Mr. Warner Van Norden, was
fɔrmed for conference with this end in view. Upon the
A nerican committee of the International Peace Congress
which met in Boston in 1904 were no less than sixteen
residents of the city of New York, — Andrew Carnegie,
Hon. Oscar S. Straus, Hon. George F. Seward, Walter
S. Logan, Felix Adler, William D. Howells, Mrs. Charles
Russell Lowell, Mrs. Anna Garlin Spencer, Miss Grace
H. Dodge, Rev. Josiah Strong, Rev. Charles E. Jeffer-
son, Cleveland H. Dodge, George Foster Peabody, Pro-
fessor John B. Clark, Leander T. Chamberlain, and J. G.
Phelps Stokes. In the week following the Boston congress a series of great peace meetings was held in New
York, at the Cooper Union and elsewhere, arranged by
members of this committee; and out of all this a new
impulse has come to plans for local organization in New
York. As one result a strong society was formed by the
Germans of the city, and a large Women's Peace Circle
has since been organized and begun important educational work. The larger New York Peace Society is
now certainly a thing of the near future. To the men
and women who will constitute that society, the noble
body of those now working in their various ways in the
great city for the cause of peace, is dedicated especially
this republication of the old essays of David Dodge, the
founder of the first peace society in the world, who by
his pioneering and prophetic service gave to New York
a place so significant in the history of what is to-day
the world's most commanding cause.

SEPTEMBER, 1905   EDWIN D. MEAD

WAR INCONSISTENT WITH THE RELIGION OF JESUS CHRIST

Humanity, wisdom, and goodness at once combine all that can be great and lovely in man. Inhumanity, folly, and wickedness reverse the picture, and at once represent all that can be odious and hateful. The former is the spirit of Heaven, and the latter the off-spring of hell. The spirit of the gospel not only breathes "glory to God in the highest, but on earth peace, and good will to men." The wisdom from above is first pure, then peaceable, gentle, easy to be entreated; but the wisdom from beneath is earthly, sensual, and devilish.

It is exceedingly strange that any one under the light of the gospel, professing to be guided by its blessed precepts, with the Bible in his hand, while the whole creation around him is so often groaning under the weight and terrors of war, should have doubts whether any kind of wars under the gospel dispensation, except spiritual warfare, can be the dictate of any kind of wisdom except that from beneath; and much more so, to believe that they are the fruit of the Divine Spirit, which is love, joy, and peace.

An inspired apostle has informed us from whence come wars and fightings. They come from the lusts of men that war in their members. Ever since the fall, mankind have had naturally within them a spirit of pride, avarice, and revenge. The gospel is directly opposed to this spirit. It teaches humility, it inculcates love, it breathes pity and forgiveness even to enemies, and forbids rendering evil for evil to any man.

Believing as I do, after much reflection and, as I trust, prayerful investigation of the subject, that all kinds of carnal warfare are unlawful upon gospel principles, I shall now endeavor to prove that WAR is INHUMAN, UNWISE, and CRIMINAL, and then make some general remarks, and state and answer several objections. In attempting to do this I shall not always confine myself strictly to this order of the subject, but shall occasionally make such remarks as may occur, directly or indirectly, to show that the whole genius of war is contrary to the spirit and precepts of the gospel.

WAR IS INHUMAN

I. BECAUSE IT HARDENS THE HEART AND BLUNTS THE TENDER FEELINGS OF MANKIND

That it is the duty of mankind to be tender-hearted, feeling for the distress of others, and to do all in their power to prevent and alleviate their misery, is evident not only from the example of the Son of God but the precepts of the gospel.

When the Saviour of sinners visited this dark and cruel world he became a man of sorrow and was acquainted with grief, so that he was touched with the feeling of our infirmities. He went about continually healing the sick, opening the eyes of the blind, unstopping the ears of the deaf, raising the dead, as well as preaching the gospel of peace to the poor. He visited the houses of affliction and poured the balm of consolation into the wounded heart. He mourned with those who mourned, and wept with those that wept. Love to God and man flowed from his soul pure as the river of life, refreshing the thirsty desert around him. He was not only affectionate to his friends but kind to his enemies. He returned love for their hatred, and blessing for their cursing. When he was surrounded by all the powers of darkness and resigned himself into the hands of sinners to expiate their guilt, and they smote him on the cheek and plucked off the hair, he "was dumb and opened not his mouth." While suffering all the contempt and torture which men and devils could invent, instead of returning evil for evil he prayed for his murderers and apologized for his persecutors, saying, "Father, forgive them, for they know not what they do."

The apostle exhorts Christians, saying, "Be ye kind and tender-hearted, forgiving one another, even as God for Christ's sake hath forgiven you."

Authority in abundance might be quoted to show that the spirit of the gospel absolutely requires the exercise of love, pity, and forgiveness, even to enemies.

But who will undertake to prove that soldiers are usually kind and tender-hearted, and that their employment has a natural tendency to promote active benevolence, while it requires all their study of mind and strength of body to injure their enemies to the greatest extent?

Though we often hear of the generosity and attention of soldiers to prisoners, and notwithstanding I am willing to allow that feelings of humanity are not altogether obliterated from every soldier, yet much of this apparent kindness may flow from a desire of better treatment themselves should circumstances be reversed, or from a hope of the applause of mankind. My object, however, is not to prove that all soldiers are destitute of humanity, but that their occupation has a natural tendency and actually does weaken their kind and tender feelings, and harden their hearts.

Is it not a fact that those who are engaged in the spirit of war, either in the council or in the field, are not usually so meek, lowly, kind, and tender-hearted as other men? Does the soldier usually become kind and tender-hearted while trained to the art of killing his fellow-man, or more so when engaged in the heat of the battle, stepping forward over the wounded and hearing the groans of the expiring? Does he actually put on bowels of tenderness, mercy, and forgiveness, while he bathes his sword in the blood of his brother? Do these scenes generally change the lion into the lamb? On the contrary, do not the history of ages and the voice of millions bear testimony that the whole trade of war has a natural tendency to blunt the tender edge of mercy and chill all the sympathizing feelings of the human heart? Who that is a parent, having an uncommonly hard-hearted and unfeeling son, would send him into the camp to subdue his inhumanity and to stamp upon him kind and tender feelings? If war has not a natural tendency to harden the heart, permit me to inquire why mankind do not usually feel as much at the distress occasioned by war as by other calamities?

It would be truly astonishing, were it not so common, to see with what composure the generality of mankind hear the account of barbarous and destructive battles. They may have some little excitement when they hear of savages — whose religion teaches them revenge — using the tomahawk and scalping knife; but when thousands are torn to pieces with shot and shells and butchered with polished steels, then it becomes a very polite and civil business, and those who perish are contemplated as only reclining on a bed of honor. If an individual in common life breaks a bone or fractures a limb, all around him not only sympathize but are ready to aid in alleviating his distress; but when thousands are slain and ten thousand wounded in the field of battle, the shock is but trifling, and the feelings are soon lost in admiring the gallantry of this hero and the prowess of that veteran. And why all this sensibility at the pains of an individual, and all this indifference at the sufferings of thousands, if war has not a natural tendency to harden the heart and destroy the tender feelings of mankind?

It is a fact, however, so notorious that the spirit and practice of war do actually harden the heart and chill the kind and tender feelings of mankind, that I think few will be found to deny it, and none who have ever known or felt the spirit of Christ.

The spirit of war must be very unlike the spirit of
the gospel, for the gospel enforces no duty the practice
of which has a natural tendency to harden men's hearts,
but in proportion as they are influenced by its spirit
and actuated by its principles they will be humane;
therefore, if war hardens men's hearts it is not a
Christian duty, and of course it cannot be right for
Christians to engage in it.

II. WAR IS INHUMAN, AS IN ITS NATURE AND TENDENCY IT ABUSES GOD'S ANIMAL CREATION

When God at first created man, he gave him authority over the beasts of the field, the fowls of the air, and
the fishes of the deep. After he had swept away the
old ungodly world of mankind for their violence with
all the animal creation, except those in the ark, he was
pleased to renew to Noah the same privilege of being
lord over the animal world.

It may not perhaps be improper here to digress a
little and remark that this appears to have been the
original bounds of man's authority, — that of having
dominion only over the animal world and not over his
fellow-man. It appears that God reserved to himself
the government of man, whom he originally created in
his own image; from which it may be inferred that
man has no lawful authority for governing his fellow-
man except as the special executor of divine command,
and that no government can be morally right except
that which acknowledges and looks up to God as the
supreme head and governor.

But to return: although the animal world is put under the dominion of man for his use, yet he has no authority to exercise cruelty towards it. "For the merciful man regardeth the life of his beast." God is very merciful to his creatures; he not only hears the young ravens when they cry but he opens his hand and supplies the wants of the cattle upon a thousand hills.

Though God has decorated the earth with beauty and richly clothed it with food for man and beast, yet where an all-devouring army passes, notwithstanding the earth before them is like the garden of Eden, it is behind them a desolate wilderness; the lowing ox and bleating sheep may cry for food, but, alas! the destroyer hath destroyed it.

The noble horse, which God has made for the use and pleasure of man, shares largely in this desolating evil. He is often taken, without his customary food, to run with an express, until, exhausted by fatigue, he falls lifeless beneath his rider. Multitudes of them are chained to the harness with scanty food, and goaded forward to drag the baggage of an army and the thundering engines of death, until their strength has failed, their breath exhausted, and the kindness they then receive is the lash of the whip or the point of a spear. In such scenes the comfort of beasts is not thought of, except by a selfish owner who fears the loss of his property.

But all this is trifling compared with what these noble animals, who tamely bow to the yoke of man, suffer in the charge of the battle; the horse rushes into the combat not knowing that torture and death are before him. His sides are often perforated with the spur of his rider, notwithstanding he exerts all his strength to rush into the heat of the battle, while the strokes of the sabers and the wounds of the bullets lacerate his body, and instead of having God's pure air to breathe to alleviate his pains, he can only snuff up the dust of his feet and the sulphurous smoke of the cannon, emblem of the infernal abode. Thus he has no ease for his pains unless God commissions the bayonet or the bullet to take away his life.

But if such is the cruelty to beasts in prosecuting war, what is the cruelty to man, born for immortality?

No wonder that those who feel so little for their fellow-men should feel less for beasts.

If war is an inhuman and cruel employment, it must be wrong for Christians to engage in it.

III. WAR IS INHUMAN, AS IT OPPRESSES THE POOR

To oppress the poor is everywhere in the Scriptures considered as a great sin: "For the oppression of the poor, for the sighing of the needy, now will I arise, saith the Lord"; "Whoso stoppeth his ears at the cry of the poor, he also shall cry himself and not be heard"; "What mean ye that ye beat my people to pieces, and grind the faces of the poor? saith the Lord God of hosts."

The threatenings against those who oppress the poor, and the blessings pronounced upon those who plead

their cause, are very numerous in the Scriptures. The
threatenings are so tremendous and awful that all men
ought to consider well before they are active in any
step which has a natural tendency to oppress the poor
and needy.

That war actually does oppress the poor may be
heard from ten thousand wretched tongues who have
felt its woe. Very few, comparatively, who are insti-
gators of war actually take the field of battle, and are
seldom seen in the front of the fire. It is usually those
who are rioting on the labors of the poor that fan up
the flame of war. The great mass of soldiers are generally from the poor of a country. They must gird on
the harness and for a few cents per day endure all the
hardships of a camp and be led forward like sheep to
the slaughter. Though multitudes are fascinated to
enlist by the intoxicating cup, the glitter of arms, the
vainglory of heroes, and the empty sound of patriotism,
yet many more are called away contrary to their wishes
by the iron hand of despotic laws. Perhaps a parent
is enrolled whose daily labor was hardly sufficient to
supply a scanty pittance for a numerous offspring, who
are in his absence crying for bread. And why all this
sorrow in this poor and needy family? Because the
husband and father is gone, and probably gone forever,
most likely to gratify the wishes of some ambitious men
who care as little as they think of his anxious family.
Perhaps an only son is taken from old, decrepit parents,
the only earthly prop of their declining years; and with
cold poverty and sorrow their gray hairs are brought
down to the dust.

War cannot be prosecuted without enormous expenses. The money that has been expended the last twenty years in war would doubtless have been sufficient not only to have rendered every poor person on earth comfortable — so far as money could do it — during the same period, but, if the residue had been applied to cultivate the earth, it would have literally turned the desert into a fruitful field. Only the interest of the money that has been expended in a few years by the European nations in prosecuting war would have been sufficient, under proper direction, to educate every poor child on earth in the common rudiments of learning, and to support missionaries in abundance to convey the gospel of peace to every creature. What a noble employment if those nations had exerted their powers for these objects as much as they have for injuring each other! And what a difference would have appeared in the world! Blessings would have fallen on millions ready to perish, instead of desolation, terror, and death.

The vast expenses of war must be met by corresponding taxes, whether by duties on merchandise or direct taxes on real estate; yet they fall most heavily on the poor. Whatever duty the merchant pays to the customhouse, he adds the amount to the price of his goods, so that the consumer actually pays the tax. If a tax is levied on real estate, the product of that estate is raised to meet it, and whoever consumes the product pays the tax. In times of war the prices of the necessaries of life are generally very much increased, but the prices of the labor of the poor do not usually rise in the same proportion, therefore it falls very heavily on them. When the honest laborers are suddenly called from the plow to take the sword and leave the tilling of the ground, either its seed is but sparingly sown or its fruit but partially gathered, scarcity ensues, high prices are the consequence, and the difficulty greatly increased for the poor to obtain the necessaries of life, especially if they were dependent on the product of a scanty farm which they are now deprived of cultivating. Many a poor widow, who has been able in times of peace to support her fatherless children, has been obliged in times of war in a great measure to depend on the cold hand of charity to supply their wants.

The calamities of war necessarily fall more on the poor than on the rich, because the poor of a country are generally a large majority of its inhabitants.

These are some of the evils of war at a distance, but when it comes to their doors, if they are favored personally to escape the ferocity of the soldiers, they fly from their habitations, leaving their little all to the fire and pillage, glad to escape with their lives, though destitute and dependent; and when they cast round their eyes for relief, they only meet a fellow-sufferer, who can sympathize with them but not supply their wants. Thus does war not only oppress the poor but adds multitudes to their number who before were comfortable.

If war actually does oppress the poor, then we may infer that in its nature and tendency it is very unlike the genius of the gospel, and not right for Christians to engage in it.

IV. WAR IS INHUMAN, AS IT SPREADS TERROR AND DISTRESS AMONG MANKIND

In the benign reign of Messiah the earth will be filled with the abundance of peace ; there will be nothing to hurt or destroy ; every one will sit quietly under his own vine and fig tree, having nothing to molest or make him afraid. But in times of war, mankind are usually full of anxiety, their hearts failing them for fear, looking for those things which are coming upon our wicked world.

One of the most delightful scenes on earth is a happy family where all the members dwell together in love, being influenced by the blessed precepts of the gospel of peace. But how soon does the sound of war disturb and distress the happy circle ! If it is only the distant thunder of the cannon that salutes the ear, the mother starts from her repose, and all the children gather round her with looks full of anxiety to know the cause. Few women can so command their feelings as to hide the cause ; and let it be said to the honor of the female sex that they have generally tender feelings, which cannot easily be disguised at the distress of their fellow-beings. Perhaps a mother's heart is now wrung with anguish in the prospect that either the partner of her life or the sons of her care and sorrow, or both, are about to be called into the bloody field of battle. Perhaps the decrepit parent views his darling son leaving his peaceful abode to enter the ensanguined field, never more to return. How soon are these joyful little circles turned into mourning and sorrow !

Who can describe the distress of a happy village suddenly encompassed by two contending armies — perhaps so early and suddenly that its inhabitants are aroused from their peaceful slumbers by the confused noise of the warriors more ferocious than the beasts that prowl in the forest? Were it not for the tumult of the battle, shrieks of distress from innocent women and children might be heard from almost every abode. Children run to the arms of their distracted mothers, who are as unable to find a refuge for themselves as for their offspring. If they fly to the streets they are in the midst of death : hundreds of cannon are vomiting destruction in every quarter; the hoofs of horses trampling down everything in their way ; bullets, stones, bricks, and splinters flying in every direction ; houses pierced with cannon shot and shells which carry desolation in their course ; without, multitudes of men rushing with deadly weapons upon each other with all the rage of tigers, plunging each other into eternity, until the streets are literally drenched with the blood of men. To increase the distress, the village is taken and retaken several times at the point of the bayonet. If the inhabitants fly to their cellars to escape the fury of the storm, their buildings may soon be wrapt in flames over their heads.

And for what, it may be asked, is all this inhuman sacrifice made? Probably to gain the empty bubble called honor, — a standard of right and wrong without form or dimensions. Let no one say that the writer's imagination is heated while it is not in the power of his feeble pen to half describe the horror and distress

of the scenes which are by no means uncommon in a
state of war.

If such are some of the effects of war, then it must
be a very inhuman employment, and wrong for Christians to engage in it.

V. WAR IS INHUMAN, AS IT INVOLVES MEN IN FATIGUE, FAMINE, AND ALL THE PAINS OF MUTILATED BODIES

To describe the fatigues and hardships of a soldier's
life would require the experience of a soldier, so that
only some of their common sufferings can be touched
upon by a person who is a stranger to the miseries of
a camp.

A great majority of those who enter the ranks of an
army are persons unaccustomed to great privations and
severe fatigues; hence the great proportion of mortality
among fresh recruits. Their habits and strength are
unable to endure the hard fare, rapid and constant
marches generally imposed upon them in active service.

The young soldier commonly exchanges a wholesome
table, a comfortable dwelling, an easy bed, for bad food,
the field for his house, the cold earth for his bed, and
the heavens over him for his covering. He must stand
at his post day and night, summer and winter; face the
scorching sun, the chilling tempest, and be exposed to
all the storms of the season, without any comfortable
repose; perhaps during most of the time with a scanty
allowance of the coarsest food, and often destitute of
any, except the miserable supply he may have chance

to plunder, — not enough to satisfy but only to keep
alive the craving demands of nature; often compelled
to march and countermarch several days and nights in
succession, without a moment to prepare his provisions
to nourish him and glad to get a little raw to sustain
his life. Frequently this hardship is endured in the
cold and inclement season, while his tattered clothing is
only the remains of his summer dress. Barefooted and
half naked, fatigued and chilled, he becomes a prey to
disease, and is often left to perish without a human
being to administer to him the least comfort. If he is
carried to a hospital, he is there surrounded by the pes-
tilential breath of hundreds of his poor fellow-sufferers,
where the best comforts that can be afforded are but
scanty and dismal.

But all this is comparatively trifling to the sufferings
of the wounded on the field of battle. There thousands
of mangled bodies lie on the cold ground hours, and
sometimes days, without a friendly hand to bind up a
wound; not a voice is heard except the dying groans of
their fellow-sufferers around them. No one can describe
the horrors of the scene: here lies one with a fractured
skull, there another with a severed limb, and a third
with a lacerated body; some fainting with the loss of
blood, others distracted, and others again crying for help.

If such are some of the faint outlines of the fatigues
and sufferings of soldiers, then their occupation must be
an inhuman employment, for they are instrumental in
bringing the same calamities on others which they suffer
themselves; and of course it is unfriendly to the spirit
of the gospel, and wrong for Christians to engage in it.

VI. WAR IS INHUMAN, AS IT DESTROYS THE
    YOUTH AND CUTS OFF THE HOPE OF GRAY
    HAIRS

Mankind are speedily hastening into eternity, and it
might be supposed sufficiently fast without the aid of
all the ingenuity and strength of man to hurry them
forward; yet it is a melancholy truth that a great proportion of the wealth, talents, and labors of men are
actually employed in inventing and using means for the
premature destruction of their fellow-beings.

One generation passes away, and another follows in
quick succession. The young are always the stay and
hope of the aged; parents labor and toil for their children to supply their wants and to educate them to be
happy, respectable, and useful, and then depend upon
them to be their stay and comfort in their declining
years. Alas, how many expectations of fond parents
are blasted! Their sons are taken away from them
and hurried into the field of slaughter.

In times of war the youth — the flower, strength, and
beauty of the country — are called from their sober, honest, and useful employments, to the field of battle; and
if they do not lose their lives or limbs, they generally
lose their habits of morality and industry. Alas! few
ever return again to the bosom of their friends. Though
from their mistaken and fascinating views of a soldier's
life and honor they may be delighted in enlisting, and
merry in their departure from their peaceful homes, yet
their joy is soon turned into pain and sorrow. Un-
thinking youth, like the horse, rushes thoughtlessly

into the battle. Repentance is then too late; to shrink
back is death, and to go forward is only a faint hope of
life, Here on the dreadful field are thousands and hundreds of thousands driven together to slaughter each
other by a few ambitious men, perhaps none of whom
are present. A large proportion are probably the youth
of their country, the delight and comfort of their
parents. All these opposing numbers are most likely
persons who never knew or heard of each other, having
no personal ill-will, most of whom would in any other
circumstances not only not injure each other but be
ready to aid in any kind office; yet by the act of war
they are ranged against each other in all the hellish
rage of revenge and slaughter.

No pen, much less that of the writer's, can describe
the inhumanity and horrors of a battle. All is confusion and dismay, dust and smoke arising, horses running,
trumpets blasting, cannon roaring, bullets whistling,
and the shrieks of the wounded and dying vibrating
from every quarter. Column after column of men charge
upon each other in furious onset, with the awful crash
of bayonets and sabers, with eyes flashing and visages
frightfully distorted with rage, rushing upon each other
with the violence of brutish monsters; and when these
are literally cut to pieces others march in quick succession, only to share the same cruel and bloody tragedy.
Hundreds are parrying the blows; hundreds more are
thrusting their bayonets into the bowels of their fellow-
mortals, and many, while extricating them, have their
own heads cleft asunder by swords and sabers; and all
are hurried together before the tribunal of their Judge,

with hearts full of rage and hands dyed in the blood of their brethren.

O horrid and debasing scene! my heart melts at the contemplation, and I forbear to dwell upon the inhuman employment.

VII. WAR IS INHUMAN, AS IT MULTIPLIES WIDOWS AND ORPHANS, AND CLOTHES THE LAND IN MOURNING

The widow and fatherless are special objects of divine compassion, and Christianity binds men under the strongest obligation to be kind and merciful towards them, as their situation is peculiarly tender and afflicting.

"A father of the fatherless, and a judge of the widow, is God in his holy habitation." "Pure religion and undefiled before God and the Father is this, to visit the fatherless and widows in their affliction."

To be active in any measure which has a natural tendency to wantonly multiply widows and orphans in a land is the height of inhumanity as well as daring impiety.

I will venture to say that no one circumstance in our world has so greatly multiplied widows and fatherless children as that of war. What has humanity ever gained by war to counterbalance simply the afflictions of the widow and fatherless? I verily believe nothing comparatively. I am well aware that a very popular plea for war is to defend, as it is styled, "our firesides, our wives and children"; but this generally is only a specious address to the feelings, to rouse up a martial spirit which makes thousands of women and children wretched where one is made happy. I am sensible that those will sneer at my opinion who regard more the honor that comes from men than they do the consolation of the widow and the fatherless.

In times of war thousands of virtuous women are deprived of their husbands and ten thousands of helpless children of their fathers. The little tender children may now gather round their disconsolate mothers, anxiously inquiring about their fathers, remembering their kind visages, recollecting how they used fondly to dandle them on their knees and affectionately instruct them; but now they are torn from their embraces by the cruelty of war, and they have no fathers left them but their Father in heaven.

It is probably no exaggeration to suppose that in Europe there are now two hundred thousand widows and a million fatherless children occasioned by war. What a mass of affliction! humanity bleeds at the thought! These children must now roam about without a father to provide for, protect, or instruct them. They now become an easy prey to all kinds of vice; many probably will be trained up for ignominious death, and most of them fit only for a soldier's life, to slaughter and to be slaughtered, unless some humane hand kindly takes them under its protection.

And here I cannot help admiring the spirit of Christianity. It is owing to the blessed spirit and temper of the gospel of peace that many of the evils of war are so much ameliorated at the present day as well as the inhuman slavery of men.

The numerous asylums that now exist for the relief of the needy, the widow, and the fatherless are some of the precious fruits of Christianity; and if this spirit were universal the bow would soon be broken to pieces, the spear cut asunder, and the chariots of war burnt with fire, and wars would cease to the ends of the earth.

And is it not the duty of all who name the name of Christ to do all in their power to counteract this destroying evil?

War not only multiplies widows and orphans but clothes the land in mourning. In times of war multitudes of people are clothed with ensigns of mourning. Here are gray-headed parents shrouded in blackness, weeping for the loss of darling sons; there are widows covered with veils mourning the loss of husbands, and refusing to be comforted; children crying because their fathers are no more. Cities and villages are covered in darkness and desolation; weeping and mourning arise from almost every abode.

And it may be asked, What inhuman hand is the cause of all this sorrow? Perhaps some rash man, in the impetuosity of his spirit, has taken some unjust, high ground, and is too proud to retrace a step, and had rather see millions wretched than to nobly confess that he had been in the wrong.

Surely Christians cannot be active in such measures without incurring the displeasure of God, who styles himself the father of the fatherless and the judge and avenger of the widow.

Thus I have shown that war is inhuman and therefore wholly inconsistent with Christianity, by proving that it tends to destroy humane dispositions; that it hardens the hearts and blunts the tender feelings of men ; that it involves the abuse of God's animal creation ; that it oppresses the poor; that it spreads terror and distress among mankind; that it subjects soldiers to cruel privations and sufferings ; that it destroys the youth and cuts off the hope of the aged ; and that it multiplies widows and orphans and occasions mourning and sorrow.

The fact that war is inhuman is indeed one of those obvious truths which it is difficult to render more plain by argument ; those who know in what war consists cannot help knowing that it is inhuman.

What Mr. Windham said with reference to the inhumanity of slavery may be said of the inhumanity of war. In one of his speeches in the House of Commons against the slave trade he stated his difficulty in arguing against such a trade to be of that kind which is felt in arguing in favor of a self-evident proposition. "If it were denied that two and two made four, it would not be a very easy task," he said, "to find arguments to support the affirmative side of the question. Precisely similar was his embarrassment in having to prove that the slave trade was unjust and inhuman."

Whoever admits that the slave trade is inhuman must admit that war is inhuman in a greater variety of ways and on a much larger scale.

The inhumanity of the slave trade was the great and, finally, triumphant argument by which it was proved to be inconsistent with Christianity.

The advocates of slavery, like the advocates of war, resorted to the Old Testament for support ; but it appeared that slavery, as it appears that war, was permitted and approved of for reasons and on principles peculiar to the ancient economy. This is apparent as well from the difference between the general design of the old and new dispensations as from the whole genius and spirit of the gospel. Hence those who opposed the slave trade argued from the general nature and spirit of Christianity as the strongest ground which could be taken. If slavery was inconsistent with this, it ought not to be tolerated ; but slavery is inhuman and is therefore inconsistent with Christianity. Exactly the same is true of war, nor can anything short of an express revelation from God, commanding war or slavery, render either of them justifiable.

It deserves to be distinctly considered that the gospel contains little or nothing directly by way of precept against slavery ; but slavery is inconsistent with its general requirements and inculcations and is therefore wrong. But war, besides being inconsistent with the genius and spirit of the gospel, is prohibited by those precepts which forbid retaliation and revenge and those which require forgiveness and good will.

It is plain, then, that he who does not advocate and defend the slave trade, to be consistent, must grant that war is incompatible with Christianity, and that it is a violation of the gospel to countenance it.

WAR IS UNWISE

That the principles and practice of war are unwise I argue:

I. BECAUSE, INSTEAD OF PREVENTING, THEY PROVOKE INSULT AND MISCHIEF

The maxim, that in order to preserve peace, mankind must be prepared for war, has become so common, and sanctioned by such high authority, that few question its wisdom or policy; but if stripped of its specious garb, it may appear to proceed not from that wisdom which came down from above, which is "first pure, then peaceable, gentle, easy to be entreated, full of mercy and good fruits, without partiality, and without hypocrisy"; and if it is not the wisdom from above, then it must be the wisdom from beneath.

Are not pride, avarice, and revenge the seeds of all kinds of carnal warfare? From these grow all the quarreling among children, the discord among families, the bickerings, law suits, and broils among neighbors, the boxing among bullies, the dueling among modern gentlemen, and wars among nations. They all originate from one and the same spirit.

Now, is the mild, meek, and peaceable man, unarmed, more liable to inspire jealousy in others that he is about to insult and abuse them than the high-toned duelist who constantly carries with him deathly weapons? Does he, in fact, so often get into difficulty, quarreling and fighting? The respectable

Society of Friends stands a living monument to answer the question.

On the principles of self-defense, as they are styled, if one man suspects an injury from another, unless he is naturally a more powerful man, he must take a cane, as the principles of self-defense require a superior power in your own hand, either by art or muscular strength. When the other learns the suspicions and sees the preparation, he in his turn must take a bludgeon to preserve the balance of power and proclaim a threatening to awe his antagonist, who must now take a sword and return a threatening in order to maintain his dignity; for it will not do for men of honor to retract, however much they may be in the wrong. The other, again, must take a deathly weapon for his defense, and nothing is now wanting but an unhappy meeting to set each other's blood a flowing.

Much in the same way do nations often get into desperate warfare. One nation is busily increasing its military strength on the plausible maxim of preserving peace and maintaining its rights. Another nation views the preparations with a jealous eye, and also goes to work on the same principle to make formidable preparations. All the nations around take the alarm, and on the same principle begin active preparations, all vying with each other to become the most formidable. If one sends an ambassador to inquire the cause of the great preparations, the answer always is, let the motive be what it may, *For their own defense.* Then the other makes new exertions and begins to fortify towns on the confines of his neighbor, who must not only do the same but

march a large army for the defense of his frontier; and
the other must do likewise. By this time, if no old quarrel remained unsettled, perhaps one charges the other
with encroachment on territory; the other denies the
charge, and contends sharply for his pretended rights.
Ministers may be interchanged, and while negotiations
are pending a high tone must be taken by both parties,
for this is an essential principle in the doctrine of self-
defense; the contrary would betray weakness and fear.
Newspapers must be ushered forth with flaming pieces
to rouse, as it is called, the spirit of the countries, so
as to impress upon the populace the idea that the ap-
proaching war is just and necessary, for all wars must
be just and necessary on both sides. In the meantime
envoys extraordinary may be sent to other powers by
each party to enlist their aid, — most of whom are
already prepared for war, —and each one selects his side
according to his interests and feelings. At length the
ultimatum is given and refused, and the dreadful conflict commences. Few wars, however, begin in this slow
and progressive mode; a trifling aggression is sufficient
to blow up the flame with nations already prepared.

Thus, we see, nations resemble bulldogs who happen
to meet. They will first raise their hairs, show their
teeth, then growl, and then seize upon each other with
all their strength and fury; and bulldogs have something of the same kind of honor, for they scorn to
retreat.

Hence we see that the acknowledged principles of
defensive war are the vital springs of most of the wars
that agitate and desolate our world. The pretended

distinction between offensive and defensive war is but a name. All parties engaged in war proclaim to the world that they only are fighting in defense of their rights, and that their enemies are the aggressors; while it may be impossible for man to decide which are most in the wrong.

The popular maxim of being prepared for war in order to be at peace may be seen to be erroneous in fact, for the history of nations abundantly shows that few nations ever made great preparations for war and remained long in peace. When nations prepare for war they actually go to war, and tell the world that their preparations were not a mere show.

Thus we may see that the principles and preparations of war actually engender war instead of promoting peace; and of course they are unwise, and, if unwise, then it is folly for Christians to engage in them.

II. WAR IS UNWISE, FOR INSTEAD OF DIMINISH- ING, IT INCREASES DIFFICULTIES

As the principles and preparations of war have a natural tendency to generate war and are actually the cause of a great proportion of the wars which do exist, so actual hostilities have a natural tendency to increase difficulties and to spread abroad the destroying evil.

It is almost impossible for any two nations to be long engaged in war without interfering with the rights and privileges of other nations, which generally awakes their jealousy and resentment, so that most of the surround- ing nations are drawn into the destructive vortex, which is the more easily done, as war inflames the martial spirit in other nations not engaged, and rouses up the desperate passions of men. Besides, the belligerent nations are not content with suffering themselves, but use every art and persuasion to get 'the neighboring nations to join them; and they are generally too successful, for it seldom happens that two nations engage in war for a length of time and conclude a peace before they have involved other nations in their difficulties and distresses, and often a great proportion of the world is in arms.

Moreover, the nations who first engage in the contest always widen the breach between themselves by war.

It is much easier settling difficulties between individuals or nations before actual hostilities commence than afterwards. Mankind are not apt to be any more mild and accommodating in a state of actual warfare. Besides, new difficulties constantly arise. The passions become inflamed, and charges are often made of violating the established laws of civilized warfare, which laws, however, are generally bounded only by the strength of power. If one party makes an incursion into the other's territory and storms a fortified place and burns the town, the other party must then make a desperate effort to retaliate the same kind of destruction, to a double degree, on the towns of their enemy. Retaliation, or "rendering evil for evil," is not only allowed by Mahometans and pagans, but is an open and avowed principle in the doctrine of self-defense among professed Christian nations; not only is it sanctioned by the laity, but too often by the priests who minister in the name of Jesus Christ.

Both of the contending parties generally seize on each other's possessions wherever they can get hold of them, whether on the seas or on the land. The barbarous spoliations on each other stir up the passions of the great mass of their inhabitants, until they esteem it a virtue to view each other as natural and perpetual enemies, and then their rulers can prosecute the war with what they call vigor.

Can the wound now be so easily healed as it could have been before it became thus lacerated and inflamed? Facts speak to the contrary, and nations seldom attempt negotiations for peace under such circumstances. They generally prosecute the war with all their power until one party or the other is overcome, or until both have exhausted their strength, and then they may mutually agree to a temporary peace to gain a little respite, when perhaps the original matter of dispute has become comparatively so trifling that it is almost left out of the account.

With a small spirit of forbearance and accommodation how easily might the difficulties have been settled before such an immense loss of blood and treasure!

If war does actually increase, instead of diminishing, difficulties, then it must be very unwise to engage in it.

III. WAR IS UNWISE, BECAUSE IT DESTROYS PROPERTY

Property is what a great proportion of mankind are struggling to obtain, and many at the hazard of their lives. Though in some instances they may misuse it, yet it is the gift of God, and when made subservient to more important things, it may be a blessing to individuals and communities. .It has in it, therefore, a real value, and ought not to be wantonly destroyed while it may be used as an instrument for benefiting mankind.

It is a notorious fact that war does make a great destruction of property. Thousands of individuals on sea and on land lose their all, for the acquisition of which they may have spent the prime of their lives. Ships on the high seas are taken, often burnt or scuttled, and valuable cargoes sent to the bottom of the deep, some possibly laden with the necessaries of life and bound to ports where the innocent inhabitants were in a state of famine. Whole countries are laid waste by only the passing of an immense army : houses are defaced, furniture broken to pieces, the stores of families eaten up, cornfields trodden down, fences torn away and used for fuel, and everything swept in its train as with the besom of destruction more terrible to the inhabitants than the storms of heaven when sent in judgment. Beautiful towns are often literally torn to pieces with shot and shells. Venerable cities, the labor and pride of ages, are buried in ashes amid devouring flames, while in melancholy grandeur the fire and smoke rise to heaven and seem to cry for vengeance on the destroyers.

Notwithstanding an avaricious individual or nation may occasionally in war acquire by plunder from their brethren a little wealth, yet they usually lose on the whole more than they gain. On the general scale the loss is incalculable. It is not my object to examine

the subject in relation to any particular nation or
war, but upon the general scale in application to all
warlike nations and all wars under the light of the
gospel.

If war does destroy property, reduce individuals to
beggary, and impoverish nations, then it is unwise to
engage in it.

IV. WAR IS UNWISE, AS IT IS DANGEROUS TO THE LIBERTIES OF MEN

Liberty is the gift of God, and ought to be dear to
every man ; not, however, that licentious liberty which
is not in subordination to his commands. Men are not
independent of God. He is their creator, preserver, and
benefactor. In his hand their breath is, and he has a
right to do what he will with his own ; and the Judge
of all the earth will do right. As man is not the
creator and proprietor of man, he has no right to
infringe on his liberty or life without his express divine
command ; and then he acts only as the executor of God.
Man, therefore, bears a very different relation to God
from what he does to his fellow-man.

The whole system of war is tyrannical and subversive
of the fundamental principles of liberty. It often brings
the great mass of community under the severe bondage
of military despotism, so that their lives and fortunes
are at the sport of a tyrant. Where martial law is proclaimed, liberty is cast down, and despotism raises her
horrid ensign in its place and fills the dungeons and
scaffolds with her victims.

Soldiers in actual service are reduced to the most abject slavery, not able to command their time for a moment, and are constantly driven about like beasts by petty tyrants. In them is exhibited the ridiculous absurdity of men rushing into bondage and destruction to preserve or acquire their liberty and save their lives.

When the inhabitants of a country are cruelly oppressed by a despotic government, and they rise in mass to throw off the yoke, they are as often as otherwise crushed beneath the weight of the power under which they groaned, and then their sufferings are greatly increased; and if they gain their object after a long and sanguinary struggle, they actually suffer more on the whole than they would have suffered had they remained in peace. It is generally the providence of God, too, to make a people who have thrown off the yoke of their oppressor smart more severely under the government of their own choice than they did under the government which they destroyed. This fact ought well to be considered by every one of a revolutionary spirit.

War actually generates a spirit of anarchy and rebellion which is destructive to liberty. When the inhabitants of a country are engaged in the peaceable employments of agriculture, manufactures, and commerce, anarchy and rebellion seldom happen. When these useful employments flourish, abundance flows in on every side, gentleness and humanity cast a smile over the land, and pleasure beams in almost every countenance. To turn the attention of a nation from these honest employments to *that of war* is an evil of unspeakable

magnitude. The great object in times of war is to
rouse up what is styled the spirit of the country, —
which, in fact, is nothing but inflaming the most destructive passions against its own peace and safety.
If you infuse into a nation the spirit of war for the
sake of fighting a foreign enemy, you do that which is
often most dangerous to its own liberties; for if you
make peace with the common enemy, you do not
destroy the spirit of war among your own inhabitants;
pride, discontent, and revenge will generally agitate the
whole body, so that anarchy and confusion will fill the
land, and nothing but a despotic power can restrain it;
and often absolute despotism is too feeble to withstand
it, and the only remedy is again to seek a common
enemy. Nations have sometimes waged war against
other nations because there was such a spirit of war
among their own inhabitants that they could not be
restrained from fighting, and if they had not a common
foe they would fight one another. So when a nation
once unsheathes the sword, it cannot easily return the
sword again to the scabbard, but must keep it crimsoned
with the blood of man until "they who take the sword
shall perish with the sword," agreeably to the denunciation of Heaven.

To inflame a mild republic with the *spirit of war* is
putting all its liberties to the utmost hazard, and is an
evil that few appear to understand or appreciate. No
person can calculate the greatness of the evil to trans-
form the citizens of a peaceful, industrious republic
into a band of furious soldiers; and yet the unhappy
policy of nations is to cultivate a martial spirit that

they may appear grand, powerful, and terrific, when in fact they are kindling flames that will eventually burn them up root and branch.

In confirmation of what has been said, if we examine the history of nations we shall find that they have generally lost their liberties in consequence of the spirit and practice of war. Thus have republics who have boasted of their freedom lost their liberty one after another, and that this has resulted from the very nature of war and its inseparable evils is evident from the fact that so violent and deadly is this current of ruin, republics have generally sunk down to the lowest abyss of tyranny and despotism, or have been annihilated and their inhabitants scattered to the four winds of heaven. Indeed, what nation that has become extinct did not first lose its liberty by war, and then hasten to its end under the dominion of those passions which war inflames?

Do nations ever enjoy so much liberty as when most free from the spirit of war? Are their liberties ever so little endangered as when this spirit is allayed and all its foreign excitements removed? Do not nations that have partially lost their civil liberties gradually regain them in proportion as they continue long without war? Is it not a common sentiment that the liberties of a people are in danger when war engrosses their attention? On the whole, is it not undeniable that peace is favorable to liberty, and that war is its enemy and its ruin? If so, what can be more unwise, what more opposite to every dictate of sound wisdom and policy, than the spirit and practice of war?

V. WAR IS UNWISE, AS IT DIMINISHES THE HAPPINESS OF MANKIND

Happiness is the professed object which most men are striving to obtain. Alas ! few, comparatively, seek it where it is alone to be found. But that happiness which flows from the benevolent spirit of the gospel is to be prized far above rubies; it is a treasure infinitely surpassing anything that can be found merely in riches, honors, and pleasures.

But war always diminishes the aggregate of happiness in the world. When nations wage war upon each other, all classes of their inhabitants are more or less oppressed. They are subjected to various privations; prosperity declines; external sources of happiness are mostly dried up; anxiety for friends, loss of relations, loss of property, the fear of pillage, severe services, great privations, and the dread of conquest keep them constantly distressed. They are like the troubled sea that cannot rest, whose waters cast up mire and dirt.

Those actually engaged in war generally suffer privations and hardships of the severest kind. Even the sage counselors who declare wars are often in so great anxiety and pain as to the result of their enterprises as to be unable quietly to refresh themselves with food or sleep.

All the rejoicings occasioned by military success are fully counterbalanced by the pain and mortification of the vanquished; and, in short, all the interest and happiness resulting from war to individuals and nations are dearly bought, and are at the expense of other individuals and nations.

It is because war has no tendency to increase, but does in fact greatly diminish, happiness that it is so universally regarded and lamented as the greatest evil that visits our world. Hence fasting has generally been practiced by warlike Christian nations to deplore the calamity, to humble themselves before God, and to supplicate his mercy in turning away the judgment.

Though fasting and deep humility before God is highly suitable for sinners, with a hearty turning away from their sins and humble supplication for God's mercy through the mediation of Christ, yet those fasts of nations who have voluntarily engaged in war and are determined to prosecute it until their lusts and passions are gratified do not appear to be such fasts as God requires.

Does it not appear absurd for nations voluntarily to engage in war, and then to proclaim a fast to humble themselves before God for its evils, while they have no desire to turn away from them, but, on the contrary, make it an express object to seek the divine aid in assisting them successfully to perpetuate it?

We often see contending nations, all of whom cannot be right, on any principle, proclaiming fasts, and chanting forth their solemn *Te Deums* as each may occasionally be victorious. Though such clashing hymns cannot mingle in the golden censer, yet few Christians seem to question the propriety of quarreling and fighting nations each in their turn supplicating aid in their unhallowed undertakings and returning thanks in case of success. Doubtless many would consider it as solemn mockery to see two duelists before their meeting supplicating

God's blessing and protection in the hour of conflict, and then to see the victor returning thanks for his success in shedding the blood of his brother; and yet, when nations carry on the business by wholesale (if I may be allowed the expression) it is considered a very pious employment. The Lord has said, "And when ye spread forth your hands, I will hide mine eyes from you : yea, when ye make many prayers, I will not hear ; your hands are full of blood."

Penitent Christians may weep and mourn with propriety for their own sins and the sins of the nations, with a hearty desire not only to forsake their own iniquities, but that the nations may be brought to confess and forsake their sins and turn from them to the living God. It is true that war is a judgment in God's providence. It is also a sin of the highest magnitude and ought to be repented of. It is a crime so provoking to Heaven that other calamities generally attend it. The famine, fire, and pestilence often attend its horrors and spread distress through a land. War with its attending evils unquestionably diminishes the aggregate of happiness in the world, and is therefore unwise.

VI. WAR IS UNWISE, AS IT DOES NOT MEND, BUT INJURES, THE MORALS OF SOCIETY

The strength, defense, and glory of a country consists primarily in the good moral character of its inhabitants. The virtuous and the good are the salt that preserve it from ruin. Says the Rev. Dr. Miller in his sermon on the death of Dr. Rogers (pages 366 and 388 of the Memoirs), "It is manifest from the whole tenor of his word that God is slow to inflict heavy judgments upon a nation in which many of his people dwell; that he often spares it, spreads over it the protection of his providence, and finally delivers it for their sake; and, of course, that the presence of his beloved children, speaking after the manner of men, is a better defense than chariots and horsemen, a better defense than all the plans of *mere* politicians, than all the skill, courage, and activity of *mere* warriors." Again, "I have no doubt that it is as great and precious a truth at this day as it ever was, that a praying people are, under God, the greatest security of a nation."

When the inhabitants of a country become generally profane and dissolute in their manners, slaves to dissipation and vice, it is usually God's providence soon to visit them in his wrath and let loose the instruments of his destroying vengeance; how important, therefore, in a temporal point of view, is the preservation of good morals to a nation. But no event has so powerful a tendency to destroy the morals of a people as that of actual war. It draws the attention of the inhabitants from useful employments; it generates curiosity, dissipation, and idleness, and awakes all the furious passions of men.

War occasions a great profanation of the Sabbath. Under God's providence the Sabbath has always been a great barrier against vice, and the observance of it is indispensable to good morals.

In time of war the Sabbath among soldiers is often a day of parade. In the streets of the best-regulated

cities may be seen soldiers marching, flags flying, drums
and fifes playing, and a rabble of children following in
the train. Now all this is not only calculated to dissi-
pate all reverential respect for the solemnities of the
day among the soldiers, but is calculated to destroy the
respect and observance of the day with which the children and youth have been inspired. Add to this, flags
are suspended from the windows of taverns and grogshops to entice in the youth by the intoxicating cup.
In the camp the Sabbath is almost forgotten and rendered a common day. Armies from professing Christian nations as often begin offensive operations on the
Sabbath as on any other day ; and professing Christians
not only tolerate all this but approve of it as a work
of necessity and mercy.

War occasions dishonesty. In countries where armies
are raised by voluntary enlistment all kinds of deception and art are practiced by recruiting officers, and
connived at by their governments, to induce the heed-
less youth to enlist. The honor and glory of the employment is held up to view in false colors ; the importance
of their bounty and wages are magnified ; the light-
ness of the duty and opportunities for amusements and
recreation are held out ; and probably one half have
the assurances of being noncommissioned officers, with
a flattering prospect of a speedy advancement ; and
prospects of plunder are also held out to their cupidity.
These deceptive motives are daily urged under the stimulating power of ardent spirits and the fascinating charms
of martial music and military finery. Many a young man
who has entered the rendezvous from curiosity or for

the sake of a dram, without the least idea of joining the army, has been entrapped into intoxication, and his hand then grasped the pen to seal his fate.

Recruits after joining the army find from experience that most of the allurements held out to them to enlist were but a deception, and from lust and want they often become petty thieves and plunderers to repay them for their great privations, fatigues, and sufferings.

War occasions drunkenness, — one of the greatest evils and most destructive to morality, as a multitude of other vices necessarily follow in its train. Many a young man has entered the military ranks *temperate*, and has returned from them a *sot*. All the enticements of liquor are exhibited in the most inviting forms to youth in the streets by the recruiting officer, to tempt them to enlist; and while those who have enrolled themselves remain at the rendezvous, they are probably every day intoxicated with the inebriating poison, soul and body, and soon the habit becomes confirmed. While in actual service their fatigues are so great that they greedily lay hold on the destroying liquor wherever they can find it to exhilarate their languid frames, even if they had not before acquired an insatiable thirst; and soon this detestable evil will become so enchanting that they will not only barter away their wages for it but their necessary clothing. If they survive the campaign and return to their homes, they are often the visitors of grogshops and taverns, and by their marvelous stories attract the populace around them, who must join them in circulating the cup; and thus they spread this destroying evil all around.

War occasions profaneness. Profaneness is an abomination in the sight of God : "For the Lord will not hold him guiltless who taketh his name in vain." Profaneness draws down the judgments of heaven, "for because of swearing the land mourneth."

That soldiers are generally considered more profane than other men is evident, because it has become a proverb that "such a person is as profane as a soldier, or a man-of-war's man." Young men who have been taught to revere the name of the God of their fathers may shudder at the awful profanations that fill their ears when they first enter an army ; but if destitute of grace in the heart, the sound will soon cease to offend, and they will eagerly inhale the blasphemous breath and become champions in impiety. For want of habit they may not swear with so easy a grace as the older soldiers ; they will for that reason make great exertions and invent new oaths, which will stimulate their fellows again to exceed in daring impiety. Seldom does a soldier return from the camp without the foul mouth of profanity. Astonishing to think that those who are most exposed to death should be most daring in wickedness !

War occasions gambling. A great proportion of the amusements of the camp are petty plays at chance, and the stake usually a drink of grog. The play is fascinating. Multitudes of soldiers become established gamblers to the extent of their ability, and often, if they return to society, spread the evil among their neighbors.

War begets a spirit of quarreling, boxing, and dueling ; and no wonder that it should, for the whole business of war is nothing else but quarreling and fighting. The soldier's ambition is to be a bully, a hero, and to be careless of his own life and the lives of others. He is therefore impatient in contradiction, receives an insult where none was intended, and is ready to redress the supposed injury with the valor of his own arms; for it will not do for soldiers to shrink from the contest and be cowards.

War destroys the habits of industry and produces idleness. Industry is necessary to good morals as well as to the wealth and happiness of a country, and every wise government will take all laudable means to encourage it; but a large proportion of common soldiers who may return from the armies have lost the relish and habits of manual labor and are often found loitering about in public places, and if they engage in any kinds of labor, it is with a heavy hand and generally to little purpose. They therefore make bad husbands, unhappy neighbors, and are worse than a dead weight in society. Their children are badly educated and provided for, and trained up to demoralizing habits, which are handed down from generation to generation.

These immoralities, and many more that might be named, are not confined to soldiers in time of war, but they are diffused more or less through the whole mass of community; and war produces a general corruption in a nation, and is therefore unwise, even in a temporal point of view. But when we consider the natural effects of these immoralities on the souls of men, all temporal advantages are in comparison annihilated. In this school of vice millions are ripening for eternal woe.

The destroying influence will spread and diffuse itself through the whole mass of society unless the spirit of the Lord lifts up a standard against it.

The state of morals, so much depressed by the American Revolution, was only raised by the blessed effusions of God's holy spirit.

If war does actually demoralize a people, then no wise person can consistently engage in it.

VII. WAR IS UNWISE, AS IT IS HAZARDING ETERNAL THINGS FOR ONLY THE CHANCE OF DEFENDING TEMPORAL THINGS

Says our blessed Saviour : " For what is a man profited, if he should gain the whole world, and lose his own soul?"

The loss of a soul infinitely exceeds all finite calculations. It is not only deprived forever and ever of all good but is plunged into misery inexpressible and everlasting. All temporal things dwindle to nothing when placed in comparison with eternal realities. The rights, liberties, and wealth of nations are of little value compared with one immortal soul. But astonishing to think that millions and millions have been put at everlasting hazard only for the chance of defending temporal things!

The habits and manners of a soldier's life are calculated, as we have already seen, to demoralize them, to obliterate all early serious impressions, to introduce and confirm them in the most daring wickedness and fit them for everlasting destruction. And notwithstanding

God may have occasionally, to display his sovereign power, snatched some soldiers from the ranks of rebellion and made them the heirs of his grace, yet no sober Christian will say that the army is a likely place to promote their salvation; but, on the contrary, must acknowledge that it is a dangerous place for the souls of men. It may be assumed as an undeniable fact that the great mass of soldiers are notoriously depraved and wicked. With but few exceptions their impiety grows more daring the longer they practice war; and when it is considered that thousands and thousands of such are hurried by war prematurely into eternity, with all their sins unpardoned, what an amazing sacrifice appears only for some supposed temporal good. But when it is remembered that this infinite sacrifice is made merely for the chance of obtaining some temporal advantage, the folly of war appears in more glaring colors, as the battle is not always to the strong. Those who are contending for their rights, and are least in the wrong, are about as often unsuccessful as otherwise, and then they very much increase their evils in a temporal point of view. A wise man would not engage in a lawsuit to recover a cent, admitting that it was his just due, if the trial put to the hazard his whole estate. But this bears no comparison with *one soul* in competition with all temporal things; and yet men, professing to be *wise*, not only put one soul at hazard but millions, not for the *chance* of defending all temporal good, but often for a mere bubble, the hollow sound of honor; and many of those who are watching for souls, and must give an account, instead of sounding the alarm, approve of it.

All who engage in war, either in the field or otherwise, practically regard *time* more than eternity, and *temporal* more than *eternal* things.

If souls are of more value than temporal things, and eternity of more consequence than time, it must be *unwise* to engage in a war and put souls to immediate hazard of everlasting ruin, and totally wrong for Christians to engage in it.

VIII. WAR IS UNWISE, AS IT DOES NOT ANSWER THE PROFESSED END FOR WHICH IT IS INTENDED

The professed object of war generally is to preserve liberty and produce a lasting peace; but war never did and never will preserve liberty and produce a lasting peace, for it is a divine decree that all nations who take the sword shall perish with the sword. War is no more adapted to preserve liberty and produce a lasting peace than midnight darkness is to produce noonday light.

The principles of war and the principles of the gospel are as unlike as heaven and hell. The principles of war are terror and force, but the principles of the gospel are mildness and persuasion. Overcome a man by the former and you subdue only his natural power, but not his spirit; overcome a man by the latter, and you conquer his spirit and render his natural power harmless. Evil can never be subdued by evil. It is returning good for evil that overcomes evil effectually. It is, therefore, alone the spirit of the gospel that can preserve liberty and produce a lasting peace. Wars can never cease until the principles and spirit of war are abolished.

Mankind have been making the experiment with war for ages to secure liberty and a lasting peace ; or, rather, they have ostensibly held out these objects as a cover to their lusts and passions. And what has been the result? Generally the loss of liberty, the overturning of empires, the destruction of human happiness, and the drenching of the earth with the blood of man.

In most other pursuits mankind generally gain wisdom by experience ; but the experiment of war has not been undertaken to acquire wisdom. It has, in fact, been undertaken and perpetuated for ages to gratify the corrupt desires of men. The worst of men have delighted in the honors of military fame and it is what they have a strong propensity for ; and how can a Christian take pleasure in that employment which is the highest ambition of ungodly men? The things that are highly esteemed among men are an abomination in the sight of God. Is it not, therefore, important that every one naming the name of Christ should bear open testimony against the spirit and practice of war and exhibit the spirit and temper of the gospel before the world that lieth in wickedness, and let their lights shine before men?

But what can the men of the world think of such Christians as are daily praying that wars may cease to the ends of the earth, while they have done nothing and are doing nothing to counteract its destructive tendency? Alas! too many are doing much by their lives and conversation to support its spirit and principles.

Can unbelievers rationally suppose such prayers to be sincere? Will they not rather conclude that they are perfect mockery? What would be thought of a man daily praying that the means used for his sick child might be blessed for his recovery, when he was constantly administering to him known poison? With the same propriety do those Christians pray that war may come to a final end, while they are supporting its vital principles.

It is contrary to fact that war is calculated to preserve liberty and secure a lasting peace; for it has done little else but destroy liberty and peace and make the earth groan under the weight of its terror and distress.

It is contrary to the word of God that war is calculated to promote peace on earth and good will toward men. The law that is to produce this happy effect will not be emitted from the council of war or the smoke of a camp; but the law shall go forth out of Zion, and the Lord shall rebuke the strong nations and they shall beat their swords into plowshares and their spears into pruning hooks; then nations shall no more lift up sword against nation, neither shall they learn the art of war any more; then shall the earth be filled with the abundance of peace and there shall be nothing to hurt or destroy. It is reserved alone for the triumph of the gospel to produce peace on earth and good will to men.

If war does actually provoke insult and mischief; if it increases difficulties, destroys property and liberty; if it diminishes happiness, injures the morals of society, hazards eternal for only the chance of defending temporal things, and, finally, does not answer the end for which it was intended, then it must be *very unwise* to engage in it, and it must be wrong for Christians to do anything to promote it, and right to do all in their power to prevent it.

WAR IS CRIMINAL

I am now to show that war, when judged of on the principles of the gospel, is highly criminal.

I. GOING TO WAR IS NOT KEEPING FROM THE APPEARANCE OF EVIL, BUT IS RUNNING INTO TEMPTATION

. . . I would have it understood that I consider every act of mankind which is palpably contrary to the spirit and precepts of the gospel *criminal.*

It is an express precept of the gospel to abstain from all appearance of evil. "Watch and pray that ye enter not into temptation" is also an express command of Christ.

A person desiring not only to abstain from evil, but from the very appearance of it, will suffer wrong rather than hazard that conduct which may involve doing wrong. He will be so guarded that if he errs at all he will be likely to give up his right when he might retain it without injuring others.

No person, it is believed, will attempt to maintain that there is no appearance of evil in carnal warfare, or that it is not a scene of great temptation.

One great object of the gospel is to produce good morals, to subdue the irascible passions of men and bring them into sweet subjection to the gospel of peace.

But war cannot be prosecuted without rousing the corrupt passions of mankind. In fact, it is altogether the effect of lust and passion. In times of war almost every measure is taken for the express purpose of inflaming the passions of men, because they are the vital springs of war, and it would not exist without them. Those who are engaged in war, both in the council and in the field, have a feverish passion, which varies as circumstances may happen to change. Those who are actually engaged in the heat of battle are usually intoxicated with rage. Should this be denied by any one, I would appeal to the general approbation bestowed on the artist who displays most skill in painting scenes of this kind. He who can represent the muscular powers most strongly exerted, the passions most inflamed, and the visage most distorted with rage, will gain the highest applause. The truth of the assertion is, therefore, generally admitted. Some men, perhaps, may be so much under the influence of pride as to have the appearance of stoical indifference when their antagonists are at some distance, but let them meet sword in hand and the scene is at once changed.

The temptations for those who constitute, or those who encourage and support, armies to commit or to connive at immorality are too various and too multiplied to be distinctly mentioned.

Who can deny that war is altogether a business of strife? But, says an inspired apostle, "where envying and strife is, there is confusion and every evil work."

Now, if war is a scene of confusion and strife and every evil work, it is impossible for any one to engage in it and avoid the appearance of evil or be out of the way of temptation; those who are armed with deathly weapons and thirsting for the blood of their fellow-mortals surely cannot be said to exhibit no appearance of evil. But if engaging in wars is putting on the appearance of evil and running into temptation, then it is highly criminal to engage in it.

II. WAR IS CRIMINAL, AS IT NATURALLY INFLAMES THE PRIDE OF MAN

One of the abominable things which proceed out of the corrupt heart of man, as represented by our Saviour, is pride. "God resisteth the proud, but giveth grace to the humble." "The Lord hates a proud look." "Every one that is proud in heart is an abomination to the Lord." That pride is criminal and that humility is commendable will doubtless be admitted by all who believe the Scriptures.

Pride, however, is one of the chief sources of war. It is pride that makes men glory in their strength and prowess; it is pride that hinders them from confessing their faults and repairing the injury done to others.

Although pride is commonly condemned in the abstract, yet it is generally commended in soldiers and fanned by every species of art and adulation, not only

by men of the world but too often by those who bear
the Christian name. And why is it necessary to inflame
the pride of soldiers? Because it is well understood
that soldiers without pride are not fit for their business.

If war is a Christian duty, why should not the example and precepts of Christ, instead of the example of
the heroes of this world, be exhibited to those who
fight to stimulate them? Is not Christ as worthy of
imitation as the Cæsars and Alexanders of this world?
He was a triumphant conqueror; he vanquished death
and hell, and purchased eternal redemption for his
people; but he conquered by resignation and triumphed
by his death. Here is an example worthy of the highest
emulation. And why not animate soldiers by it? Only
because it would unnerve their arms for war and render
them harmless to their foes.

It is so common to compliment the pride of soldiers
that, instead of considering it that abominable thing
which the Lord hates, they consider it a virtue. We
frequently hear "gentlemen of the sword," as they are
styled, in reply to the flattery bestowed upon them,
frankly declare that it is their highest ambition to obtain
the praise of their fellow-citizens; and, of course, they
confess that they are seeking the praise of men more
than the praise of God. These gentlemen, however,
are far less criminal than those who lavish flattery on
them; for doubtless most of them are sincere and think
themselves in the way of their duty, while their profession often leads them, necessarily, from the means
of knowing correctly what is duty. While professing
Christians have been taught from their cradles that the

profession of arms is not merely an allowable but a noble employment, it is easy for them to slide into the current and go with the multitude to celebrate victories and to eulogize heroes, without once reflecting whether they are imitating their Lord and Master. But is it not time for Christians to examine and ascertain if war is tolerated in the gospel of peace before they join in festivities to celebrate its bloody feats? How would a pagan be astonished if he had been taught the meek, lowly, and forgiving spirit and principles of the gospel, without knowing the practice of Christians, to see a host of men, professing to be influenced by these blessed principles, marshaled in all the pomp of military parade, threatening destruction to their fellow-mortals! Would he not conclude that either he or they had mistaken the genius of the gospel, or that they believed it to be but a fable?

It is a notorious fact, which requires no confirmation, that military men, decorated with finery and clad in the glitter of arms, instead of being meek and lowly in their temper and deportment, are generally flushed with pride and haughtiness; and, indeed, what purpose do their decorations and pageantry answer but that of swelling their vanity? Their employment is not soft and delicate. Other men who follow rough employments wear rough clothing; but the soldier's occupation is not less rough than the butcher's, though, in the world's opinion, it is more honorable to kill men than to kill cattle.

But if war has a natural tendency to inflame, and does inflame and increase the pride of men, it is criminal; it does that which the Lord hates, and it must be highly criminal to engage in it.

III. WAR NECESSARILY INFRINGES ON THE CON-
SCIENCES OF MEN, AND THEREFORE IS
CRIMINAL

Liberty of conscience is a sacred right delegated to man by his Creator, who has given no authority to man to infringe in the least on the conscience of his fellow-man. Though a man, by following the dictates of his conscience, may be injured by men, yet they have no authority to deprive him of the rights of conscience. To control the conscience is alone the prerogative of God. That man has no right to violate the conscience of his fellow-man is a truth which few, under the light of the gospel, since the days of ignorance and superstition, have ventured to call in question.

But military governments, from their very nature, necessarily infringe on the consciences of men. Though the word of God requires implicit obedience to rulers in all things not contrary to the Scriptures, it utterly forbids compliance with such commands as are inconsistent with the gospel. We must obey God rather than man, and fear God as well as honor the king. But governments, whether monarchial or republican, make laws as they please, and compel obedience at the point of the sword. They declare wars, and call upon all their subjects to support them.

Offensive war, by all professing Christians, is considered a violation of the laws of Heaven; but offensive war is openly prosecuted by professing Christians under the specious name of self-defense. France invaded Spain, Germany, and Russia; England invaded

Holland and Denmark; and the United States invaded Canada, under the pretense of defensive war. The fact is, however, that no man can, on gospel principles, draw a line of distinction between offensive and defensive war so as to make the former a crime and the latter a duty, simply because the gospel has made no such distinction. But while many Christians profess to make the distinction, and to consider offensive war criminal, they ought to have the liberty to judge, when war is waged, whether it is offensive or defensive, and to give or withhold their aid accordingly; otherwise they are not permitted the free exercise of their consciences.

But suppose this principle adopted by governments. Could they prosecute war while they left every individual in the free exercise of his conscience to judge whether such war was offensive or defensive and to regulate his conduct accordingly? Would it be possible for governments to carry on war if they depended for support on the uncertain opinion of every individual? No; such a procedure would extinguish the vital strength of war and lay the sword in the dust. The fact is well known, and monarchs declare war and force their subjects to support it. The majority in republican governments declare war and demand and enforce obedience from the minority.

Though the constitutions of governments may, in the most solemn manner, guarantee to citizens the free exercise of their consciences, yet governments find it necessary practically to make an exception in relation to war, and a man may plead conscientious motives in vain to free himself from contributing to the support of war.

I think it proper here to notice what has appeared to me a gross absurdity among some Christians in this land. They have openly declared that in their opinion the late war was offensive; that it was contrary to the laws of God, and that they were opposed to it; but though they wished not to support it because it was criminal, yet they said, if they were called on in a constitutional way, they would support it. Thus did they publicly declare that they would, under certain circumstances, obey man rather than God.

But soldiers actually resign up their consciences to their commanders, without reserving any right to obey only in such cases as they may judge not contrary to the laws of God. Were they at liberty to judge whether commands were morally right or not, before they yielded obedience, it would be totally impracticable for nations to prosecute war. Ask a general if his soldiers have the privilege of determining whether his commands are right or not, and he will tell you it is their duty only to obey.

Suppose that a general and his army are shut up in a city in their own country, and that provisions are failing; that an army is advancing for their relief, but cannot reach the place until all means of sustenance will be consumed; that the inhabitants cannot be let out without admitting the besiegers; and that in this extremity, to preserve his army for the defense of his country, the commander orders his men to slay the inhabitants, doing this evil that good may come. But some conscientious soldiers refuse to obey a command to put the innocent to the sword for any supposed good. What must be the consequence? Their lives must answer for their disobedience. Nor is this contrary to the usages of war. And Christians satisfy their consciences upon the false principle that soldiers are not accountable for their conduct, be it ever so criminal, if they obey their commanders; all the blame must fall on the officers, which involves the absurdity of obeying man rather than God. Thus soldiers must be metamorphosed into something besides moral and accountable beings in order to prosecute war; and, in fact, they are treated generally not as moral agents but as a sort of machinery to execute the worst of purposes.

The only plausible method of which I can conceive to avoid the above consequences requires that soldiers should not practically resign their consciences, but, when commands which are morally wrong are given, that they should refuse obedience and die as martyrs. But to enter an army with such views would be to belie the very oath of obedience which they take. Besides, who could execute the martyrs and be innocent? In this way all might become martyrs, and the army be annihilated.

But if war does not admit the free exercise of conscience on Christian principles, then it is criminal for Christians to become soldiers, and the principles of war must be inconsistent with the principles of Christianity.

IV. WAR IS CRIMINAL, AS IT IS OPPOSED TO PATIENT SUFFERING UNDER UNJUST AND CRUEL TREATMENT

That patient suffering under unjust and cruel treatment from mankind is everywhere in the gospel held up to view as the highest Christian virtue probably few professing Christians will deny.

But notwithstanding this truth is generally admitted, there is very commonly introduced a carnal, sophistical mode of reasoning to limit, or explain away, this precious doctrine, which is peculiar to the gospel and which distinguishes it from all other kinds of morality and religion on earth. It has relation, it is said, only to matters of religion and religious persecution, — as if the gospel required mankind actually to regard a little wealth and a few temporal things more than all religious privileges and life itself ; for, by this human maxim, men may fight to defend the former, but not the latter. And this maxim is built on the supposition that Christians are not bound strictly by gospel precepts in relation to temporal things, but only in relation to spiritual things. Hence it is said that the martyrs conducted nobly in refusing to fight for the privilege of worshiping the true God, but if Christians now refuse to fight to defend their money and their political freedom they act in a dastardly manner and violate the first principles of nature. Thus are temporal regarded more than spiritual and everlasting things.

The precepts of the gospel, however, unequivocally forbid returning evil for evil, and enjoin patient

sufferings under injurious and cruel treatment. A few
instances shall be quoted : " Now we exhort you, brethren, warn them that are unruly, comfort the feeble-
minded, support the weak, be patient towards all men.
See that none render evil for evil to any man; but ever
follow that which is good, both among yourselves, and
unto all men." " If, when ye do well, and suffer for it,
ye take it patiently, this is acceptable with God." The
apostle James, in his solemn denunciation against oppressors, says, "Ye have condemned and killed the just,
and he doth not resist you"; he then immediately
exhorts the Christians, saying, " Be patient therefore,
brethren, unto the coming of the Lord." " Finally, be
ye all of one mind, having compassion one for another,
love as brethren, be pitiful, be courteous, not rendering evil for evil, railing for railing; but contrariwise
blessings, knowing that ye are thereunto called, that ye
should inherit a blessing." " For the eyes of the Lord
are over the righteous, and his ears are open to their
prayers ; but the face of the Lord is against them that
do evil. And who is he that will harm you, if ye be
followers of that which is good?"

A patient, forbearing, suffering disposition is peculiar to the lamblike temper of the gospel, and is wholly
opposed to the bold, contending, daring spirit of
the world which leads mankind into quarreling and
fighting.

It is generally admitted, I believe, that it is the duty
of Christians patiently to suffer the loss of all temporal
things, and even life itself, rather than willfully violate
any of God's commands. If, then, it is the duty of a

Christian patiently to suffer death rather than bear false witness against his neighbor, be he friend or foe, is it not equally his duty patiently to suffer death rather than kill his neighbor, whether friend or foe? Not merely taking away the life of our neighbor is forbidden, but every exercise of heart and hand which may have a natural tendency to injure him. But which is the greatest evil, — telling a lie, or killing a man? By human maxims you may do the latter to save your life, but not the former; though the former might injure no one but yourself, while the latter, besides injuring yourself, might send your neighbor to eternal destruction.

The spirit of martyrdom is the true spirit of Christianity. Christ himself meekly and submissively died by the hands of his enemies, and instead of resistance, even by words, he prayed, " Father, forgive them, for they know not what they do." Stephen, when expiring under a shower of stones from his infuriate murderers, prayed, " Lord, lay not this sin to their charge." St. Paul testified that he was not only ready to be bound but to die for the Lord Jesus. The early martyrs resigned up their lives with patient submission as witnesses for Jesus, — and this at a time, when, Sir Henry Moncrief Wellwood in his Sermons, page 335, says, " Tertullian has told us that Christians were sufficiently numerous to have defended themselves against the persecutions excited against them by the heathen, if their religion had permitted them to have recourse to the sword."

The spirit of martyrdom is the crowning test of Christianity. The martyr takes joyfully the spoiling of his goods, and counts not his life dear to himself.

But how opposite is the spirit of war to the spirit of martyrdom! The former is bold and vindictive, ready to defend property and honor at the hazard of life, ready to shed the blood of an enemy. The latter is meek and submissive, ready to resign property and life rather than injure even an enemy. Surely patient submission under cruel and unjust treatment is not only the highest Christian virtue but the most extreme contrast to the spirit of war.

Now if it is a duty required by the gospel not to return evil for evil, but to overcome evil with good; to suffer injustice and to receive injury with a mild, patient, and forgiving disposition, — not only in words but in actions, — then all kinds of carnal contention and warfare are criminal and totally repugnant to the gospel, whether engaged in by individuals or by communities.

Can it be right for Christians to attempt to defend with hostile weapons the things which they profess but little to regard? They profess to have their treasure not in this world but in heaven above, which is beyond the reach of earthly invaders, so that it is not in the power of earth or hell to take away their dearest interests. There may be a propriety in the men of the world exclaiming that their dearest rights are invaded when their property and political interests are infringed upon; but it is a shame for Christians to make this exclamation, while they profess to believe that their dearest interest is in the hand of Omnipotence, and that the Lord God of hosts is their defense.

Whoever, without divine command, dares to lift his hand with a deathly weapon against the life of his fellow-man for any supposed injury denies the Christian character in the very act, and relies on his own arm instead of relying on God for defense.

V. WAR IS CRIMINAL, AS IT IS NOT DOING TO OTHERS AS WE SHOULD WISH THEM TO DO TO US

Says our blessed Saviour, "All things whatsoever ye would that men should do to you, do ye even so to them; for this is the law and the prophets." Now if we wish men to be kind and forbearing to us, we must be kind and forbearing to them; if we wish them to return love for hatred and good for evil, then we must return love for hatred and good for evil; if we wish not to be injured by men, then we must not injure them; if we wish not to be killed, then we must not kill.

But what is the practical language of war? Does the man who is fighting his fellow-man and exerting all his strength to overcome him really wish to be overcome himself and to be treated as he is striving to treat his enemy? Can it be believed that England, in the late war, wished France to do to her what she endeavored to do to France; or that the latter really desired in return what she endeavored to inflict on England? If not, both violated this express precept of Christ.

None can say, consistently with the principles of the gospel, that they wish to be killed by their enemies; therefore none can, consistently with those principles, kill their enemies. But professing Christians do kill their enemies, and, notwithstanding all they may say to the contrary, their actions speak louder than their words. It is folly for a man to say he does not wish to do a thing while he is voluntarily exerting all his powers to accomplish it.

But if the act of war does violate this express precept of Christ, then it must be exceedingly criminal to engage in it.

VI. WAR IS INCONSISTENT WITH MERCY, AND IS THEREFORE CRIMINAL

Mercy is the grand characteristic of the gospel, and the practice of mercy is the indispensable duty of man. " Be ye merciful, as your Father also is merciful "; "For he maketh his sun to rise on the evil and on the good, and sendeth rain on the just and on the unjust "; " Blessed are the merciful, for they shall obtain mercy "; " For he shall have judgment without mercy, that hath showed no mercy."

Mercy is that disposition which inclines us to relieve distress, to forgive injuries, and to promote the best good of those who are ill deserving. Mercy in us towards our enemies implies seeking and pursuing their best good for time and eternity. It is sinful to exercise any affection towards enemies short of that benevolence or mercy which involves the advancement of their best good, and Christians may not suspend this disposition, or do evil that any supposed good may come; for no law can be of higher authority than the express precept of

Christ which requires this disposition towards enemies, and of course no other consideration can be paramount to this, for nations are as much bound as individuals.

It is surely too grossly absurd for any to pretend that destroying the property and lives of enemies is treating them mercifully, or pursuing their best good for time and eternity. Nor can any so impose upon their imaginations as to think that injuring mankind is treating them with benevolence or mercy.

But the direct object of war is injury to enemies; and the conduct of soldiers generally speaks a language not easily to be misunderstood. Though soldiers are not always as bad as they might be, their tender mercies are often but cruelty. When they storm a fortified place and do not put all the captives to the sword, they are complimented for exercising mercy, merely because they were not so cruel as they might have been. But shall a highway robber be called an honest man because he takes but half the money of him whom he robs? Is it an act of mercy, when a man encroaches on your property, to take away his life? Do nations exercise mercy towards each other when they enter into bloody wars in consequence of a dispute which shall govern a small portion of territory? or does a nation show mercy to another that has actually invaded its rights by falling upon the aggressor and doing all the injury in its power? This surely is not forgiving injuries. And when two contending armies come in contact and rush on each other with all the frightful engines of death and cut each other to pieces they do not appear to me as merciful, kind, and tender-hearted, forgiving one another in love, even as God for Christ's sake forgives his children. Yet this is the rule by which they should act and by which they will at last be judged.

But the whole system of war is opposed to mercy, and is therefore altogether unlike the spirit of the gospel, and must be criminal.

VII. WAR IS CRIMINAL, AS THE PRACTICE OF IT IS INCONSISTENT WITH FORGIVING TRESPASSES AS WE WISH TO BE FORGIVEN BY THE FINAL JUDGE

Our Saviour says: "If ye forgive men their trespasses, your heavenly Father will also forgive you; but if ye forgive not men their trespasses, neither will your heavenly Father forgive your trespasses"; "Forgive, and ye shall be forgiven."

Here it is evident that the everlasting salvation of men depends on their exercising forgiveness towards their enemies; for if they forgive not, they will not be forgiven of God, and with what measure they mete to others, it will be measured to them again.

To forgive is to pass by an offense, treating the offender not according to his desert, but as though he had done nothing amiss.

But do the principles of war lead individuals or nations to pass by offenses and to treat offenders as if they were innocent? Do they not, on the contrary, require justice and exact the very last mite? Has it the aspect of forgiveness for us, when an enemy trespasses on our rights, to arm with weapons of slaughter

and meet him on the field of battle? Who, while pier-
cing the heart of his enemy with a sword, can consistently utter this prayer: "Father, forgive my trespasses,
as I have forgiven the trespasses of this my enemy"?
But this, in reference to this subject, is the only prayer
the gospel warrants him to make. And professing
Christian nations, while at war and bathing their swords
in each other's blood to redress mutual trespasses, are
daily in their public litanies offering this prayer ; but
is it not obvious that either their prayers are perfect
mockery, or they desire not to be forgiven but to be
punished to the extent of their deserts ?

If individuals or nations desire that God would forgive their trespasses, then they must not only pray for
it, but actually exercise forgiveness towards those who
trespass against them ; and then they may beat their
useless swords into plowshares and their spears into
pruning hooks and learn war no more.

But it must be very criminal to engage in war, or to
tolerate it in any way, if it is inconsistent with the forgiveness of injuries as we hope to be forgiven, and in
this respect violates the precepts of the gospel.

VIII. ENGAGING IN WAR IS NOT MANIFESTING LOVE TO ENEMIES OR RETURNING GOOD FOR EVIL

Returning good for evil and manifesting benevolence
to enemies is, perhaps, the most elevated and noble part
of Christian practice, — the inculcation of which in the
gospel exalts Christianity far above any other form of

religion and proves it to be not only divine but effica-
cious to subdue the turbulent and corrupt passions of
men; and for these reasons this part of duty ought to
be zealously advocated and diligently performed by every
one who bears the Christian name.

The ablest writers who have defended the divine
origin of the Scriptures against infidels have urged this
topic as constituting conclusive evidence in their favor;
and unbelievers, instead of attempting to meet the argument fairly, have urged the inconsistency of Christians
in acting contrary to so conspicuous a rule of duty; and
such is and ever has been the most powerful weapon
that infidels can wield against Christianity. But it is
the will of God that by welldoing we should put to
silence the ignorance of foolish men. Let Christians
act in strict conformity to this part of Christian practice, and they will wrest from the infidel's hand his
strongest weapon.

That exercising benevolence towards enemies and
returning good for evil is inculcated as one of the most
important doctrines of the gospel is evident as well
from the whole tenor of the New Testament as from
the express commands of the Son of God : " I say unto
you, Love your enemies, bless them that curse you, do
good to them that hate you, and pray for them that
despitefully use you and persecute you, that ye may be
the children of your Father in heaven "; " If thine
enemy hunger, feed him ; if he thirst, give him drink ;
for in so doing thou shalt heap coals of fire on his
head "; " Be not overcome of evil, but overcome evil
with good."

Such are some of the divine precepts on this subject.
So different, however, are the laws of war among Christian nations, that rendering comfort or relief to enemies
is considered high treason, and they punish with death
the performance of the very duty which God commands
as a condition of eternal life !

The common sense of every man revolts from the
idea that resisting an enemy by war is returning good
for evil. Who would receive the thrust of a sword as
an act of kindness? Was it ever considered that killing
a man was doing good to him? Has not death always
been considered the greatest evil which could be returned for capital crimes? But the principles of war
not only allow enemies to return evil for evil by killing
one another, but secure the highest praise to him who
kills the most. It is often said of those who distinguish
themselves in butchering their fellow-men, that "they
cover themselves with glory !"

Nations, when they go to war, do not so much as
pretend to be actuated by love to their enemies ; they do
not hesitate to declare in the face of Heaven that their
object is to *avenge* their wrongs. But, says an inspired
apostle, "Dearly beloved, avenge not yourselves, but
give place unto wrath : for it is written, Vengeance is
mine ; I will repay, saith the Lord." Retributive judgment, the execution of strict justice, or vengeance, God
declares often, belongs to him. He has reserved it in
his own hand as his sovereign prerogative.

It is not very surprising that savage pagans should
glory in revenge, but that those should do so who have
the Bible in their hands, and profess to take it as the

rule of their faith and practice, is truly astonishing.
Still more astonishing is it that some ministers of the
gospel not only connive at but approve of the spirit
and practice of revenge by war.

But though the whole tenor of the gospel absolutely
enjoins returning good for evil and blessing for cursing;
yet the open and avowed principles of war are to return
evil for evil, violence for violence.

Now if the principles of war are so directly opposed
to the principles of the gospel, if the practice of war is
so perfectly contrary to Christian practice, then it must
be very criminal for Christians not to bear open testimony against war, and much more criminal to do
anything to promote it.

IX. WAR IS CRIMINAL, BECAUSE IT IS ACTUALLY RENDERING EVIL FOR EVIL

It is a fact which can neither be disguised nor controverted that the whole trade of war is returning evil
for evil. This is a fundamental principle in the system
of self-defense. Therefore every exertion in the power
of contending nations is made to inflict mutual injury,
not merely upon persons in public employment and upon
public property, but indiscriminately upon all persons
and property. Hence it is an established rule of what is
styled "civilized warfare" that if one party takes a person
suspected of being a spy, they put him to death; which
act is retaliated by the other the first opportunity. If
one party storms a fortified place and puts the garrison
or the inhabitants to the sword, the other, in their

defense, must retaliate the same thing, and, if possible, to a greater degree. If one side executes a number of captives for some alleged extraordinary act, the other, on the principles of self-defense, may execute double the number; the first may then, on the same principles, double this number; and so they may proceed to return evil for evil, till one or the other yields.

The principles of self-defense require not merely an eye for an eye and a tooth for a tooth, but for one eye two eyes, for one tooth two teeth. They require the retaliation of an injury to a double degree, — otherwise, there would be no balance in favor of the defensive side; but as both parties must always be on the defense, both must, of course, retaliate to a double degree. Thus war is aggravated and inflamed, and its criminality raised to the highest pitch.

The doctrine of retaliation is not only openly avowed and practiced by professing Christian nations, but is sometimes defended before national councils by professing Christians of high standing in churches. "O! tell it not in Gath! publish it not in the streets of Askelon! lest the daughters of the uncircumcised triumph!"

That the retaliation of injury, of whatever kind it may be and to whomsoever it may be offered, is most absolutely and unequivocally forbidden by the whole spirit of the gospel dispensation, as well as by its positive precepts, surely can never be fairly controverted.

Says the great Author and finisher of our faith, "Ye have heard that it hath been said, An eye for an eye, and a tooth for a tooth: but I say unto you that ye resist not evil; but whosoever shall smite thee on the right cheek, turn to him the other also." Whether the literal import of these words be contended for or not, they cannot fairly be construed as teaching anything short of a positive and unconditional prohibition of the retaliation of injury. Had our Lord added to these words the maxim of the world, " If any man assaults you with deathly weapons, you may repel him with deathly weapons," it would have directly contradicted the spirit of this command and made his sayings like a house divided against itself.

The apostles largely insist upon this doctrine of their divine Master, thus : " Recompense to no man evil for evil"; " Be ye all of one mind, not rendering evil for evil, or railing for railing "; " See that none render evil for evil to any man." These comprehensive passages make no conditions or limitations, and are, therefore, applicable to all men and binding upon all in all situations and circumstances under the light of the gospel ; but had they added, " If any man injures you, you may return him an injury and repel violence with violence," it would have been most palpably absurd, and the precepts of the gospel would have been truly what infidels have asserted they are,—a series of gross contradictions.

But I repeat that the open and avowed principles of war, even among Christian nations, are those of returning evil for evil. Surely, nations neither aim nor pretend to aim at the best good of their enemies; but, on the contrary, their real and professed object in the sight of God and man is to do them, while at war, all the injury in their power. What means that language which conveys instructions to those who command

ships of war, to *sink*, *burn*, and *destroy*, if it does not
mean evil to enemies? Why do nations encourage the
cupidity of men by licensing and letting loose swarms
of picaroons on their enemies, if it is not to inflict evil
on them? But all this is sanctioned under the notion
of self-defense, and, as though it were a light thing for
men thus publicly to trample on the laws of the gospel,
they lift up their daring hands to heaven and supplicate
God's help to assist them in violating his own commands! No apology can be made for such proceedings
until it is shown that war is not returning evil for evil.

But what is it to return evil for evil?

When one man is injured by another and returns
injury, he returns evil for evil and violates those precepts of the gospel which have been quoted. When one
association of men is injured by another association
and the injured returns an injury, evil is returned for
evil and those precepts are violated. When one nation
infringes on the rights of another and they in return
infringe on the aggressor's rights, they return evil for
evil and violate those precepts. When one nation
declares war against another and is repelled by war,
evil is returned for evil and those precepts are violated. But these things are constantly practiced, without a blush or a question as to their propriety; and
God is supplicated to aid in the business.

To what a state has sin reduced our world? Is not
the church covered with darkness and the people with
gross darkness? A man may now engage in war with
his fellow-man and openly return evil for evil, and still
remain in respectable standing in most of the churches,

being at the same time highly applauded and caressed by the world lying in wickedness !

But if we are here to be directed and at last to be judged by the gospel, no man can return evil for evil, in war or otherwise, without aggravated guilt.

X. WAR IS CRIMINAL, AS IT IS ACTUALLY DOING
   EVIL THAT GOOD MAY COME; AND THIS
   IS THE BEST APOLOGY THAT CAN BE MADE
   FOR IT

That it is an evil to spread distress, desolation, and misery through a land and to stain it with the blood of men probably none will deny. War, with its attending horrors, is considered by all, even those who advocate and prosecute it, to be the greatest evil that ever befalls this wicked, bleeding, suffering world.

Though men go to war primarily to gratify their corrupt passions, — for they can never propose the attainment of any good by war which shall be commensurate with the natural and moral evils that will be occasioned by the acquisition, — yet the prospect of attaining some supposed good must be held out as a lure to the multitude and a means of self-justification.

Usually the object of war is pompously represented to be to preserve liberty, to produce honorable and lasting peace, and promote the happiness of mankind; to accomplish which, liberty, property, and honor — that honor which comes from men — must be defended, though war is the very thing that generally destroys liberty, property, and happiness, and prevents lasting peace.

Such is the good proposed to be attained by the certain and overwhelming evil of war.

But no maxim is more corrupt, more false in its nature, or more ruinous in its results than that which tolerates doing evil that good may come. Nor can any defend this maxim without taking the part of infidels and atheists, to whom it appropriately belongs, and with whose principles and practice alone it is consistent.

The apostle Paul reprobates this maxim in the severest terms, and he considered it the greatest scandal of Christian character to be accused of approving it : "As we be slanderously reported," says he, "and as some affirm that we say, Let us do evil that good may come; whose damnation is just."

Now if war is in fact an evil, and it is prosecuted with a view to attain some good, then going to war is doing evil that good may come. It is therefore doing that which scandalizes Christian character; that which is wholly irreconcilable with the principles of the gospel, and which it is highly criminal for any man or nation to do.

XI. WAR IS OPPOSED TO THE EXAMPLE OF THE SON OF GOD, AND IS THEREFORE CRIMINAL

The example of the Son of God is the only perfect model of moral excellence, and his moral conduct, so far as he acted as man, remains a perfect example fo. Christians.

But did he appear in this world as a great military character, wearing a sword of steel, clothed with military finery, and surrounded by glittering soldiers, marching in the pomp and parade of a warrior? No; he was the meek and lowly Jesus, despised and rejected of men. He was King of kings and Lord of lords, but his kingdom was not of this world. Had his kingdom been of this world, then would he have appeared as an earthly conqueror, and his servants would have been warriors.

Though a prince, he was the Prince of Peace. At his advent the angels sang, "Glory to God in the highest, on earth peace, good will to men." "He came not to destroy men's lives, but to save them." He was the Lamb of God, meek and lowly. He followed peace with all men; he returned good for evil and blessing for cursing, and "when he was reviled he reviled not again." Finally, he was "brought as a lamb to the slaughter, and as a sheep before her shearers is dumb, so he opened not his mouth." That he did this as a necessary part of his mediatorial work need not be denied; but that he intended it also as an example to his followers is fully confirmed by an inspired apostle, who says, "If, when ye do well, and suffer for it, ye take it patiently, this is acceptable with God. For hereunto were ye called: because Christ also suffered for us, leaving us an example, that ye should follow his steps: who did no sin, neither was guile found in his mouth: who, when he was reviled, reviled not again; when he suffered, threatened not; but committed himself to him who judgeth righteously."

Christ taught his disciples the doctrines of peace, and commanded them to take up the cross and follow him; to live in peace and to follow peace with all men.

His last gift to them was peace. He said to them, when
about to send them into the world, " Behold I send you
forth as lambs among wolves "; thus teaching them
what treatment they might expect and what character
they must maintain among wicked men. The nature
of lambs and wolves is too well known for any one to mis-
take this figurative representation. Wolves are fierce,
bloody, and ravenous beasts; but lambs are mild, inoffensive, and unresisting, having no means of relief
but by flight. Now if a host of professing Christian
warriors, marshaled under the ensign of a preying eagle
or a prowling lion, clothed in all the splendor of deathly
armor, and rushing forward to destroy their fellow-crea-
tures, are in figurative language but *lambs*, I confess I
am at a loss where to look for the *wolves!* Do these
warlike Christians appear mild as lambs and harmless
as doves, kind and tender-hearted, doing good to all,
to friends and foes, as they have opportunity? Can
fighting be living peaceably with all men? Is it returning good for evil, and overcoming evil with good? If
not, it is not imitating the example of Christ.

If Christians were like Christ, their warfare would
not be carnal, but spiritual, corresponding with the
armor which he has provided. They would conquer by
faith and overcome by the blood of the Lamb, not
counting their lives dear to themselves.

On the whole, if to engage in war is not avoiding the
appearance of evil, but is running into temptation; if
it inflates the pride of men; if it infringes on the rights
of conscience; if it is not forgiving trespasses as we
wish to be forgiven; if it is not patient suffering under

unjust and cruel treatment; if it is not doing to others as we would have them do to us; if it is not manifesting love to enemies and returning good for evil; if it is rendering evil for evil; if it is doing evil that good may come; and if it is inconsistent with the example of Christ, then it is altogether contrary to the spirit and precepts of the gospel and is highly criminal. Then Christians cannot engage in war or approve of it without incurring the displeasure of Heaven.

In view of the subject, if what has been said is in substance correct, and of this I desire the reader conscientiously to judge, then the criminality of war and its inconsistency with the gospel are undeniable.

It is admitted by all that war cannot exist without criminality somewhere, and generally where quarreling and strife are, there is blame on both sides. And how it is that many Christians who manifest a laudable zeal to expose and counteract vice and wickedness in various other forms are silent on the subject of war, silent as to those parts or practices of war which are manifestly and undisputably criminal, is to me mysterious. There has been a noble and persevering opposition against the inhuman and cruel practice of the slave trade; and by the blessing of God the efforts against it have been successful, probably, for the time, beyond the most sanguine expectations. When the lawfulness of this practice was first called in question, it was violently defended as well by professing Christians as by others. Comparatively few Christians fifty years ago doubted the propriety of buying and holding slaves;

but now a man advocating the slave trade could hardly hold in this vicinity a charitable standing in any of the churches. But whence has arisen so great a revolution in the minds of the mass of professing Christians on this subject? It has happened not because the spirit or precepts of the gospel have changed, but because they are better understood.

Christians who have been early educated to believe that a doctrine is correct, and who cherish a respect for the instructions of their parents and teachers, seldom inquire for themselves, after arriving at years of maturity, unless something special calls up their attention; and then they are too apt to defend the doctrine they have imbibed before they examine it, and to exert themselves only to find evidence in its favor. Thus error is perpetuated from generation to generation until God, in his providence, raises up some to bear open testimony against it; and as it becomes a subject of controversy, one after another gains light, and truth is at length disclosed and established. Hence it is the solemn duty of every one, however feeble his powers, to bear open testimony against whatever error prevails, for God is able from small means to produce great effects.

There is at present in many of our churches a noble standard lifted up against the abominable sin of intemperance, the greatest evil, perhaps, war excepted, in the land, and this destructive vice has already received a check from which it will never recover unless Christians relax their exertions. But if war is a greater evil than drunkenness, how can Christians remain silent respecting it and be innocent?

Public teachers consider it to be their duty boldly and openly to oppose vice. From the press and from the pulpit they denounce theft, profaneness, Sabbath breaking, and intemperance; but war is a greater evil than all these, for these and many other evils follow in its train.

Most Christians believe that in the millennial day all weapons of war will be converted into harmless utensils of use, that wars will cease to the ends of the earth, and that the benign spirit of peace will cover the earth as the waters do the seas. But there will be then no new gospel, no new doctrines of peace; the same blessed gospel which we enjoy will produce "peace on earth and good will to men." And is it not the duty of every Christian now to exhibit the same spirit and temper which will be then manifested? If so, let every one "follow the things that make for peace," and the God of peace shall bless him.

OBJECTIONS ANSWERED

As was proposed, a number of objections to the general sentiments that have been advocated shall be stated and answered.

Objection first. Shall we stand still and suffer an assassin to enter our houses without resistance and let him murder ourselves and families?

Answer. I begin with this because it is generally the first objection that is made to the doctrine of peace by all persons, high and low, learned and unlearned;

notwithstanding it is an objection derived from a fear of consequences and not from a conviction of duty, and might with the same propriety have been made to the martyrs who, for conscience' sake, refused to repel their murderers with carnal weapons, as to Christians who, for conscience' sake, refuse at this day to resist evil. No Christian will pretend that defense with carnal weapons is not criminal, if the gospel really forbids it, let the consequences of nonresistance be what they may. For the requisitions of the gospel are the rule of duty. But I presume the objection above stated arises altogether from an apprehension of consequences rather than from regard to duty.

Every candid person must admit that this objection is of no force, until the question whether the gospel does or does not prohibit resistance with deathly weapons is first settled. It might, therefore, justly be dismissed without further remark; but as mankind are often more influenced by supposed consequences than by considerations of duty, and as the objection is very popular, it may deserve a more particular reply.

In the first place, I would observe that the supposition of the objector relates to a very extreme case, a case which has very rarely, if ever, occurred to Christians holding to nonresistance with deathly weapons, and it bears little or no resemblance to the general principles or practices of war which are openly advocated and promoted by professing Christians. Should an event like that supposed in the objection take place, it would be a moment of surprise and agitation in which few could act collectedly from principle. What

was done would probably be done in perturbation of
mind. But war between nations is a business of calcu-
lation and debate, affording so much time for reflection
that men need not act from sudden and violent impulse,
but may act from fixed principle. In this respect, therefore, war is a very different thing from what is involved
in the objection which does not in the least affect the
principles or practice of systematic warfare. It is not
uncommon to hear persons who are hopefully pious,
when pressed by the example and the precepts of
Christ against war, acknowledge that most of the wars
which have existed since the gospel dispensation cannot be justified on Christian principles; yet these very
persons are never heard to disapprove of the common
principles of war, or to counteract them by their lives
and conversation before a wicked world; but, on the
contrary, they will often eulogize heroes, join in the
celebration of victories, and take as deep an interest in
the result of battles as the warriors of this world; and
if their conduct is called in question, they will attempt
to justify it by pleading the necessity of self-defense,
and immediately introduce the above objection which
is by no means parallel with the general principles and
practices of all wars.

The truth is, war is a very popular thing among mankind, because it is so congenial to their natural dispositions; and, however gravely some men may, at times,
profess to deplore its calamity and wickedness, it is too
evident that they take a secret pleasure in the approbation of the multitude and in the fascinating glory of
arms; and we have reason to believe that this objection

is often made merely to ward off the arrows of conviction which would otherwise pierce their consciences.

The objection, however, wholly overlooks the providence and promise of God. Assassins do not stroll out of the circle of God's providence. Not only is their breath in his hand, but the weapons they hold are under his control. Besides, God's children are dear to him, and he shields them by his protecting care, not suffering any event to befall them except such as shall be for his glory and their good. Whoever touches them touches the apple of his eye. He has promised to be a very present help to them in every time of need, and to deliver them that trust in him out of all their trouble. He will make even their enemies to be at peace with them. For the eyes of the Lord are over the righteous and his ears are open to their prayers, but the face of the Lord is against them that do evil ; and who is he that will harm you if ye be followers of that which is good ? But if ye suffer for righteousness' sake, happy are ye, and be not afraid of their terror, neither be troubled. If God be thus for his children, who can be against them ? Is not the arm of the Lord powerful to save, and a better defense to all who trust in him than swords and guns ? Whoever found him unfaithful to his promises or feeble to save ? Are not the hosts of heaven at his command ? Are not his angels swift to do his will? " Are they not all ministering spirits sent forth to minister for them who shall be heirs of salvation ? " " The angel of the Lord encampeth round about them that fear him, and delivereth them." If the Lord is on their side, Christians have no cause to

fear what man can do unto them. Says the blessed
Saviour, "Whosoever will save his life shall lose it,
and whosoever shall lose his life for my sake shall
find it."

If consequences are rightly examined, they may
prove to be of more importance than at first supposed.
If the gospel does forbid resistance with deathly
weapons, then he who saves his temporal life by killing
his enemy may lose his eternal life ; while he who loses
his life for Christ's sake is sure of everlasting life.
Thus the Christian, if he is killed, goes to heaven; but
the assassin, if he is killed, goes to hell, and the soul of
the slayer is in danger of following. Whoever kills
another to prevent being killed himself, does it on presumption ; for, whatever may be the appearances, God
only can know whether one man will assassinate another,
before the event has taken place. Men, however, seem to
think little of killing or being killed by fighting, whether
in single combat or on the field of general battle, though
they shudder at the idea of being put to death by an
assassin, unless they can inflict or attempt to inflict on
him the same evil.

But the objection is usually made on the supposition
that the doctrine in question requires Christians to
stand still and rather court the dagger than otherwise.
This is an unfair statement, for it would be presumption
to stand still when there was a chance of escape.
Besides, the Christian must act on the defensive, not
with carnal, but with spiritual weapons, which are
more powerful when exercised in faith than swords
or spears.

Probably no instance can be found of robbers murdering such as conscientiously held to nonresistance. It is resistance that provokes violence ; forbearance and good will repress it. But if instances of this kind may be found, it is no evidence against the doctrine in question any more than against the principles of the Martyrs. God may, for wise reasons, call away some of his children by the hands of murderers ; if so, instead of losing, they save their lives.

Objection second. Self-defense, and, if necessary, with deathly weapons, is the first law of nature. All the animal creation are armed with means of defense, and the principles of the gospel are not contrary to the principles of nature ; therefore self-defense is not inconsistent with Christianity.

Answer. It is admitted that the laws of the gospel are not contrary to the primitive laws of nature ; but it is by no means granted that they are consistent with the laws of corrupt nature. In consequence of the revolt of man the earth was cursed for his sake. It appears probable that before the fall of man animals were harmless and docile ; and it is not improbable that when the curse shall be removed, when the earth shall be filled with righteousness and peace, the lion and the lamb may literally lie down together. At present, indeed, the dove, the lamb, and some other animals have no means of defense, unless flight be considered such. And while warriors are figuratively represented by ferocious beasts, real Christians are represented by lambs and doves. So far as nature is made to speak fairly on the subject, it speaks in favor of the doctrine which has been advocated.

But corrupt nature strongly dictates many things quite contrary to the precepts of the gospel; and no doctrine will be given up more reluctantly by corrupt nature than that of the lawfulness of war, because no doctrine is more congenial with the depraved feelings and propensities of unsanctified men, for their "feet are swift to shed blood; destruction and misery are in their ways, and the way of peace have they not known; there is no fear of God before their eyes."

Objection third. The precepts of the gospel are consistent with the moral law, or the eternal nature of things, which is forever the standard of right and wrong to all moral beings in the universe; and war has been prosecuted consistently with this rule of right and wrong; therefore war cannot be contrary to the precepts of the gospel.

Answer. This is an objection founded on an undefinable something aside from divine precept; yet as some terms in it have been much used in polemic divinity by men of eminent talents and piety, whose praise is in the churches, I think it neither proper nor modest to dissent from so high authority without offering some reasons. I shall, therefore, make a few general observations on what is called the moral law, the eternal rule of right and wrong, or the nature of things; all of which phrases, I believe, have been occasionally used by eminent writers as conveying the same ideas.

I cannot agree with such as suppose that a moral law or nature of things exists independently of the will of God and is the common law of God and man. It appears to me as inconsistent to suppose a law to exist without a lawgiver as to suppose a world to exist without a creator. If God is the only eternal and independent Being in the universe, and if all things are the work of his power and goodness, then the supposition that an eternal law exists independently of him appears to me to be absurd, as on this supposition there exists a law without a lawgiver and an effect without a cause. If God is not the author of all things, then there must be more than one eternal cause of things.

To suppose that the reason and fitness of things independently of the will of God, either in his works, his providence, or word, can be a rule of man's duty appears to me as inconsistent as to suppose that men might institute divine worship from such fitness of things independently of the existence of God; for the will of God to man seems as necessary to lay a foundation of moral obligation and to direct man's obedience as the existence of God is necessary to lay a foundation of religious worship. Should it be asked whether the laws of God are not founded on the eternal nature and fitness of things, I would answer that such a supposition appears to me no more reasonable than to suppose that his power is founded on the eternal capacity of things; for the capacity of things has just as much reality and eternity in it to found the omnipotence of God upon, as the reason and nature of things have to found his infinite wisdom or justice upon.

I therefore dissent from all standard of moral obligation which are supposed to exist aside from, and independently of, the divine will; and fully agree with the Assembly's Shorter Catechism, in the answer to this question : " What is the duty which God requires of man? Answer: The duty which God requires of man is obedience to his revealed will." Should it, however, be said that things do exist aside from the divine will, that it does not depend on the divine will, but on the nature of things, that two and two make four, or that a thing cannot be in motion and at rest at the same time, it is by no means admitted that this order or constitution of things exists independently of God ; but it is believed to be as much the effect of his power and goodness as anything else. And if God is not the author of all the laws both in the natural and moral world, it may reasonably be inquired, who is?

If God is the moral governor of the world, then all his laws over men, as moral beings, must be moral laws ; and to make a distinction between the laws designed to regulate the moral conduct of men, and to call some of them moral and others by different names, seems to me not necessary, while I find no such distinction in the Scriptures. Because some of God's laws were intended to be temporary, under certain circumstances, they were no less of a moral nature on that account ; neither was it any less criminal to violate them.

As created things are in some respects constantly changing, and as the relations of things are often varied, so a law may be relatively right at one time and relatively wrong at another. But as man is frail and short-sighted, and is incapable of seeing the end from the beginning, he is totally unable of himself to judge what is and what is not right, all things considered ; hence the necessity of a revelation from God to direct his steps.

That there is a fitness of things and a standard of
moral right and wrong cannot be denied; but, instead
of being founded in a supposed nature of things independent of God, it originates in the very nature and perfections of God himself, and can never be known by
man any farther than the nature and perfections of
God are known. A standard of right and wrong independent of God, whether by the name of moral law or
nature of things, is what never has been and never can
be intelligibly defined. It is like a form without dimensions, like a foundation resting on nothing. It is, therefore, in my opinion, as extravagant to talk of an eternal
nature of things, without reference to the laws of God,
as it would be to talk of an eternal wisdom or an eternal
omnipotence, independent of the existence of God.

But if the statement of the objector is meant only to
imply a rule of right and wrong emanating from the
nature and perfections of God, and coincident with his
laws, then, admitting the propriety of the terms moral
law, nature of things, etc., the objection, if it proves
anything, may prove quite too much for its advocates;
for under certain circumstances it has been consistent
with this rule of moral right and wrong utterly to exterminate nations, to destroy men, women, and children,
and show them no mercy.

Besides, the whole force of the objection rests on the
supposition that no laws which have existed, and which
were not contrary to the moral law, can be abrogated
under the Christian dispensation or be inconsistent
with the precepts of the gospel. It hence follows that
whatever has been morally right and lawful for men to

do must forever remain right and lawful to be done. This is a necessary result from the premises; but no Christian can consistently subscribe to this. The premises must, therefore, be unsound and the objection of no force.

If literal sacrifices, slavery, and many other practices which are totally abolished under the Christian dispensation were not contrary to the moral law under the Old Testament economy, why may not the same be true of war? Why may not the gospel forbid war as consistently as it can forbid slavery?

Objection fourth. The nature of religion and morality under the ancient dispensation was the same as under the new. Love to God and man was the substance of the law and the prophets; and though truth under the former was inculcated more by types and ceremonies, yet the essence of religion was the same under that as under the present dispensation; and as war was not inconsistent with the nature and precepts of religion then, it cannot be inconsistent with the nature and precepts of religion now, under like circumstances.

Answer. It is readily admitted that the essence of religion is the same under the present as under the former dispensation, both requiring at all times and in all actions holy exercises of heart in cordial obedience to divine command; yet the laws for external conduct under the two dispensations differ widely, and the practice of war involves much of the external conduct of men. It was never right for men to indulge unholy feelings in the act of war, but the external act was required as a means of executing the divine vengeance;

the gospel does not command, but seems plainly to forbid, the external act of war.

But to suppose that saints under the gospel can ever be placed in circumstances like those of the ancient church is to suppose that they may be put under the same typical economy which has vanished away, given place to the substance, and ceased to be binding even on the natural Israelites. To be in like circumstances they must also be made the executors of God's wrath, to inflict vengeance, by his particular command, on idolatrous and rebellious nations. The Israelites had the same high authority to exterminate the Canaanites and subdue the idolatrous nations about Palestine that the holy angels had to destroy Sodom and Gomorrah.

It is perfectly plain that if God should positively command Christians to take the weapons of war and not only repel invasion but actually exterminate nations, it would be their duty to obey, and a refusal would be open rebellion against God. The Old Testament saints received such commands, but Christians have no such authority, which makes a material difference in circumstances.

Some general observations relative to the different dispensations of the church of God may illustrate this topic more fully.

The Old Testament economy has sometimes, perhaps without reason, been divided into the Adamic, Patriarchal, and Mosaic dispensations of the church; but as the latter was more full and complete, and as the distinction between the Mosaic and Christian dispensations is common, I shall confine my remarks chiefly to that distinction, though I consider the great distinction to be between the Old and New Testament economies.

The Old Testament economy, in general, was typical of the New. Under the former dispensation literal and temporal things typified spiritual and everlasting things under the latter. The nation of Israel, chosen and separated from all other nations, typified the true Israel of God, who are chosen out of every nation and sanctified and set apart as a holy nation and peculiar people, to offer up spiritual sacrifices to God. The land of Canaan was a type of the heavenly Canaan. Jerusalem was a type of the New Jerusalem from above. Mount Zion and the royal throne of Israel, which were in Jerusalem, typified the heavenly Zion and the throne of the true David who now reigns in glory. The sacrifices were types of spiritual offerings. The Israelites had enemies within and foes without, literal weapons of war and literal warfare, typical of spiritual foes, spiritual armor, and spiritual warfare.[1] Their kings were seated on the throne of the Lord (see 1 Chron. xxix. 23). At the command of God they judged and made war and conquered their enemies and thus typified the· Son of God who is now on the throne of his Father

---

[1] Says the Rev. Dr. Scott, in his Essay, p. 422 : " We ought not therefore to fear our enemies because he will be with us, and if God be for us, who can be against us ? Or who can doubt but he that is in us is greater than he that is in the world ? This was typically intimated in the promises made to Israel respecting their wars with the Canaanites and other nations, which were shadows and figures of the good fight of faith." Bishop Horne, in his preface to the Psalms, views the subject in the same light.

David, and who in righteousness judges and makes war
and rides forth conquering and to conquer. The ancient
promises and threatenings were mostly temporal, but
typical of spiritual and everlasting promises and threatenings. Doubtless the gospel was preached by types
and figures under the Old Testament economy, and the
saints of old looked upon those temporal things merely
as shadows representing a more enduring substance.
When they looked upon Canaan, the land of promise,
they viewed it as a type of the heavenly Canaan, and
confessed that they were strangers and pilgrims on
earth seeking a better country. When they looked
on the bleeding lamb they beheld, by the eye of
faith, the Lamb of God who taketh away the sins of
the world.

Thus we may see that almost the whole of the Old
Testament economy was typical and temporary, and
not intended to be perfect and everlasting. But under
the gospel dispensation we have a new covenant and
better promises which are intended to be perfect and
everlasting. It is therefore more proper for those
who live under this new and perfect dispensation to
look at the substance than at the shadow for a rule of
duty. Errors are often and easily propagated by reasoning from analogy and introducing it as proof of sentiments instead of illustration. This is frequently done
in relation to the Old Testament economy and common
political government. It is not uncommon to hear ministers, in their political sermons, reason and infer just
as if there were a perfect parallel between the Jewish
theocracy and political governments, when at the head

of one was the Lord of hosts and at the head of the others are but men; when one was the church of the living God, and the others are but human institutions. They not unfrequently speak of God's driving out the heathen before his American Israel and planting them in a goodly land, as though there were a perfect parallel between the Americans driving the Indians from their native soil and taking possession of it themselves, without divine commission, and the Israelites going at the express command of God and taking possession of Canaan. Thus they endeavor to keep up a parallel between God's ancient church and civil governments. The economy of God's ancient covenant people was by no means a political institution in the popular sense, but it was a dispensation of the church of God, and in its rites, ceremonies, and government was typical of the kingdom of Messiah under his mediatorial reign, and differed widely in its nature, origin, and design from mere political governments; therefore all reasoning drawn from a supposed analogy between them is specious and false. The Israelites had no authority to enact laws or to alter God's laws one iota; their duty was implicitly to obey them.

But if Christians take their authority for going to war from the practice of the Old Testament saints, their example will prove too much; it will not only allow war, but *offensive war* in its most dreadful forms.

Objection fifth. Abraham went to war, not like the Israelites at the command of God, yet he met with the divine approbation when he returned from the slaughter of the kings; he, therefore, must have acted on a

universal law still in force; and as Christians are called
the children of Abraham they ought, of course, to imitate his example in such things as God approved.

Answer. Abraham, like the Israelites, was under a
typical dispensation and practiced rites and ceremonies
which were a shadow of good things to come. That he
acted without divine command, in the war referred to, is
more than we are warranted to say. He was a prophet
and the friend of God and probably was acquainted with
the divine will on this subject.

Christians are not called the children of Abraham
because they imitate his example in war, but because
they exercise like precious faith with him. If Christians are warranted to imitate the example of Abraham
in all things which were tolerated by God, then they
may sacrifice cattle, practice polygamy, and buy and
hold slaves. But if they object to his example as a rule
of duty in these instances, why not object to his example
as a rule of duty in the case of war?

But to say that he acted from some universal law
still in force is taking for granted the question in dispute, and cannot be admitted without evidence.

The war waged by Abraham against the kings was,
I apprehend, offensive rather than defensive; for Lot,
his brother's son, whom he rescued, did not then belong
to his family or kingdom, but was separated from him
and was also a patriarch, a father of nations, and a
prince or head over his own house or kingdom.

It appears very evident that offensive as well as
defensive war was tolerated under the patriarchal economy, as may be seen from the words of the inspired

Jacob when blessing his sons (Gen. xlviii. 22). That, as well as the Mosaic dispensation, was typical, and doubtless war was allowed under both for the same reasons.

But there can be no doubt that whoever attempts to justify war by the example of Abraham may equally justify the slavery of our fellow-men; and whoever depends on his example for authority for engaging in war, to be consistent, must advocate and defend the doctrine of slavery.

Objection sixth. It appears to be a universal law of God that "whoso sheddeth man's blood, by man shall his blood be shed." If one man, or one nation, attacks another and sheds his blood, his own must be shed in return. Hence this precept not only authorizes taking away the life of a murderer, but authorizes nations to repel by war nations that wage war against them.

Answer. Whether this was a precept given to man as a rule of duty or not is very questionable, though it has generally been so construed, at least since the dark ages of the church; and it is still more questionable whether it is a universal and perpetual law.

If we attend to the phraseology of this decree of God, we shall find it to be very different from that of the precepts, generally, delivered to Moses. God did not say to Noah, as he often did to Moses, thou shalt do this, or that, but he said, "*I will require the life of man,*" etc. If God had designed to delegate executive authority to Noah and his descendants to execute retributive judgment on the manslayer, the connection of the whole language must have been altered, for God

declared what he would do himself. It appears, therefore, to have been God's *decree*, and the promulgation
of *his* law by which he would inflict righteous judgment on the guilty; the penalty was intended as a
warning to deter mankind from violence, the sin for
which the old world was swept away. And I see no
reason why this threatening should not be considered
parallel with the decrees of Christ,—that "all they
that take the sword shall perish with the sword; he
that leadeth into captivity shall go into captivity;
he that killeth with the sword must be killed with the
sword; here is the faith and the patience of the saints."
Why the former should be considered as a rule of
obedience for man, and these latter passages not so, I
am unable to say. "He that killeth with the sword must
be killed with the sword" is as positive as "whoso
sheddeth man's blood, by man shall his blood be shed."

It may be observed that the faith and patience of the
saints is here spoken of in such a way as to imply that
they exercised and manifested their faith and patience
when they were put to death by violence or carried into
captivity. And, indeed, how could their faith and
patience appear if they, like the wicked world, returned
evil for evil, carried into captivity, and killed with the
sword?

The original threatening has been fulfilled by the
providence, and sometimes by the express command, of
God. As Noah was the head of the new world and
the father of nations, it seems to have had reference to
nations rather than to individuals; and all nations that
have shed blood in war must, in their turn, have their

own blood shed; so that all they that take the sword may perish with the sword agreeably to the threatening made known to Noah, and to those announced by Christ.

But, admitting that the law quoted in the objection was intended as a rule of duty for man, it does not appear that it was designed to be universal and perpetual. Before the flood no authority appears in any sense to have been delegated to man to shed the blood of man. So far from executing the penalty of death or causing it to be executed upon Cain, who was of the wicked one and slew his brother, notwithstanding his guilty forebodings, God threatened a sevenfold vengeance on him who should presume to do it.

Under the Mosaic dispensation many crimes were punishable with death according to positive precept; but God, for wise reasons, did not always have the penalty executed. David was guilty of murder and adultery, both capital crimes; yet he was permitted to live.

All kinds of vindictive punishment under the Christian dispensation appear to be absolutely forbidden. By vindictive I mean that which is intended to vindicate the law, as executing strict justice, and prevent offenses only, as taking away life, but which is not designed to promote the individual good of the person punished. That punishment which is designed and which has a tendency to promote the good of the punished, as well as to deter offenders, I consider to be strictly disciplinary or corrective, and consistent with the spirit and precepts of the gospel. Says an apostle, "Dearly beloved, avenge not yourselves, but give place unto wrath: for it is written, Vengeance is mine; I will

repay, saith the Lord." "For the wrath of man worketh
not the righteousness of God." It has been said that
this only forbids a revengeful temper, but this evasion
will not do ; for Christians are here forbidden to do the
very thing which God declares he will do himself, and
he does nothing but what is holy.

"Render to no man evil for evil," is a positive precept without any limitation, and which admits of no
evasion ; and it must plainly rescind the law of shedding man's blood because he had shed the blood of man.

But the exclamation is often made, What, not punish a murderer with death ! Little do those who make
this exclamation think that they themselves also are
sinners and that every sin deserves not only temporal
death but God's wrath and curse forever, and that they
are in like condemnation unless redeemed by the blood
of the Lamb. For such, it might be well to inquire if
they know "what manner of spirit they are of."

The most prominent characteristic of Messiah's reign
over men in this world is mercy, since he has secured
the rights and honor of the divine government by the
sacrifice of himself so that the guilty may live. He has
given his life as a ransom and taken the world into his
hands as the ruler, judge, and rewarder, and offers the
chief of sinners mercy; and the merits of his blood are
sufficient to cleanse from all sin as well against man as
against God. And who can help being astonished at
the amazing difference between his laws and his dealings with men, and those sanguinary laws of men
according to which under the light of the gospel they
punish with death.

The professed principle and design of these laws is strict justice; but were men dealt with according to strict justice by him who rules above, who would be able to stand? These laws of men accept no atonement for capital offenses; no mercy is offered, for none is provided for those who incur their penalty; but the gospel offers mercy to the chief of sinners while it condemns those who reject the offers. Capital offenders will never be condemned by civil governments for the rejection of offered mercy, for no mercy is provided for them. How unlike the divine government! But Christians are commanded to be merciful, as their Father in heaven is merciful, who showers down blessings on the evil and unthankful. Our Master has told us that with what judgment we judge we shall be judged; and with what measure we mete it shall be measured to us again; that if we forgive we shall be forgiven; and if we forgive not we shall not be forgiven; and that if we show no mercy we shall have judgment without mercy.

Christians ought to ponder the subject well before they advocate the consistency and safety of dispensing justice without mercy. Let them learn what that meaneth, "I will have mercy and not sacrifice."

Objection seventh. "Every purpose is established by counsel, and with good advice make war"; "For by wise counsel thou shalt make war," etc. Here war is recognized as a duty under certain circumstances, and the manner in which it is to be undertaken is pointed out, viz., by wise counsel.

Answer. The inspired Proverbs are maxims of wisdom illustrated, for the most part, by some familiar subject that existed at the time they were delivered. The object here is not to inculcate the lawfulness of war but the necessity of sound wisdom in relation to the actions of men; and the subject of war appears to be introduced merely to illustrate this idea. The counsel and wisdom of men in relation to their temporal and worldly concerns are often worthy of imitation in reference to spiritual things; for the children of this world are, in some sense, wiser in their generation than the children of light, and the conduct of worldly men is often very appropriately introduced to illustrate Christian duty. Our Lord says, "What king, going to war with another king, sitteth not down first, and consulteth whether he be able with ten thousand to meet him that cometh against him with twenty thousand?" Doubtless our Lord's design was to warn people to count the cost before they professed to be followers of him, that they might not be deceived and discouraged, and that they might act from principle and not from hypocrisy. But he inculcated these things by referring to the example of kings in their consultations about war. And it is believed that the passages before cited are of similar import. These references to war, being introduced merely for the illustration of other subjects, will no more prove the lawfulness of war than the reference of the apostle to the Olympic games, for illustration, will prove the lawfulness of those heathen feats. But if this explanation should not be satisfactory, it may be observed that the Proverbs were written under the Old Testament economy which tolerated offensive as well as defensive war; whence it does not appear that any war can be undertaken under the present dispensation, "by wise counsel," except that which is spiritual; so that if the ancient was typical of the new dispensation, then the passages quoted will now apply only to spiritual warfare.

Objection eighth. When the soldiers demanded of John the Baptist what they should do, one of the directions which he gave them was to be content with their wages. If their occupation had been unlawful, then he would not have directed them to be contented with the wages of wickedness.

Answer. John the Baptist was under the Mosaic economy, the new dispensation not having commenced. He was but the forerunner of the Lord, a herald to sound his approach. But he gave the soldiers another direction, viz., to "do violence to no man," obedience to which is totally incompatible with war, as that is nothing else but violence. Only hinder soldiers from doing violence to any man and you stop at once the whole progress of war; therefore, if the directions of John are insisted on as gospel authority, they will prove, probably, much more against the lawfulness of war than in favor of it.

Objection ninth. The Centurion and Cornelius were Christians and soldiers and highly approved of God for their faith and piety; nor were they directed by Christ or his apostles to renounce their profession; therefore the profession of arms is not inconsistent with Christian duty.

Answer. They were first soldiers and then Christians; and we have no evidence that they continued in the profession of arms; nor are we warranted to say that they were not directed to renounce that profession, as the Scriptures are silent on the subject. Peter, it appears, tarried a number of days with Cornelius, and he doubtless explained to him the spirit and precepts of the gospel; and it is very probable that neither Cornelius nor the Centurion continued soldiers in any other sense than they were soldiers of Christ, as the idolatrous rites enjoined on the Roman soldiers were totally inconsistent with the Christian character, aside from the unlawfulness of war itself. Besides, the Roman soldiers were as often engaged in offensive as in defensive war; therefore, if the argument has any force on the question, it will tolerate not only defensive but offensive war, and also the idolatrous rites of the Roman armies.

Objection tenth. Our Lord paid tribute money, which went to support military power, but he would not contribute to the support of a wicked thing, therefore war is not inconsistent with Christianity.

Answer. A distinguished trait of the Christian religion is peace. The command is, " Follow peace with all men." " Blessed are the peacemakers: for they shall be called the children of God."

Our Lord set the example of giving no just cause of offense to any. Tribute was demanded of him unjustly according to the existing laws, but lest fault should be found, he wrought a miracle and paid it. Money is a temporal thing, and belongs to the governments of this world, as the various coins bear the ensign of the nation by whom they were made; but the Christian's treasure is not in this world, and when the rulers of this world

call for that which bears their own image and super-
scription, Christians have no right to withhold from
them their dues, for they must "render to Cæsar the
things that are Cæsar's." For this cause they ought to
pay tribute and resign up temporal things without a
murmur to temporal governments, and leave it with
Cæsar to manage the things of Cæsar. Thus far are
Christians warranted to act, from the example of Christ
and the precepts of the gospel; but how does the lawfulness of war follow from Christians rendering to
Cæsar his due? Is it because some of the money goes
to support war? Probably, of the money which our
Lord paid as much went to the support of idolatry and
the games of the day as to the support of war. Now
if the argument is sound, we may not only prove by it
the lawfulness of war but the lawfulness of idolatry
and many other abominable things practiced by the
heathen governments.

Objection eleventh. Our Lord, just before his cruci-
fixion, commanded his disciples to take swords, and, if
any were destitute, to sell their garments and procure
them, as they would no longer have his personal presence to protect them; and as they were to encounter
great trials and difficulties, they must, besides relying
on providence, take all prudent means for their defense
and preservation.

Answer. That our Lord did not direct them to take
swords for self-defense is evident because he told them
that two were enough, and because the disciples never
made any use of them after their Master directed Peter
to put up his and pronounced a penalty on all who

should have recourse to swords afterwards. But the design seems to have been to show by example in the most trying situation where self-defense was justifiable, if in any case, that the use of the sword was utterly prohibited under the gospel economy, and to show the criminality and danger of ever using deathly weapons against mankind afterwards. If Christ's kingdom had been of this world, then, he tells us, his servants would have fought; but his kingdom being not of this world, the weapons of their warfare were not carnal but spiritual. He therefore rebuked them for their mistaken zeal, healed the wound they made, and forbade the use of the sword.

Objection twelfth. Christians are commanded to be in subjection to civil rulers who are God's ministers to execute wrath on the wicked and are ministers of good to the church; therefore Christians are bound to take the sword at their command; for civil government is ordained of God and civil rulers are not to bear the sword in vain, and Christians may lawfully do what God ordains to be done.

Answer. That civil government, so called in distinction from religious government, is ordained by God is fully admitted, and also that God ordains whatsoever comes to pass. But there is a great difference between his decretive and his preceptive will. The former is not a rule of duty for man without the latter; the latter is always a rule of duty. This fact might be proved by a multitude of instances from Scripture. Persons therefore may be very wicked in doing what God ordains to be done, if they act without his command.

That civil governments and civil rulers exist only by God's decretive will, which is fulfilled by his providence and not by his preceptive will, is evident because God has never authorized the appointment of them or given any precepts or any commands as a code of laws to any denomination or class of people as such, distinct from his own covenant people or church; and this fact I beg leave to submit as a conclusive evidence that civil governments and civil rulers exist only by God's decretive will and not by his preceptive will. Under the ancient dispensation no laws or directions were given to any class of men, as such, other than God's own covenant people or church, unless some special commands on singular occasions, or the general command to repent and turn to God, be excepted.

The king on the throne of Israel was as truly an officer in the church of God as the high priest who entered into the holy of holies. Both were set apart and anointed with the holy oil, at the command of God, and both were types of the Son of God. The king as much typified his kingly office as the priest did his priestly office. Both were necessary parts of that complete shadow of good things then to come.

Under the gospel dispensation no authority from God is to be found for appointing and setting apart civil rulers, nor are there any directions given to civil rulers, *as such*, how to conduct in their office, unless those who rule in the church are called civil rulers. All the precepts and directions in the gospel, excepting such as were special (as those which related only to the apostles) or such as are universal (relating alike to all

men), are given to the disciples as members of Christ's
kingdom, who are not of this world, even as he was not
of this world.

The Son of God came into the world to set up the
kingdom of heaven, which is a perfect and everlasting
kingdom and distinct from all other kingdoms which
are to be destroyed to give place to his divine and
heavenly reign. He came in the likeness of men, sin
excepted, and laid down his life a ransom for the
world, and then rose a triumphant conqueror, and in the
complex character of God and man, as Mediator, he
took the universe, his purchased possession, into his
hands as a lawgiver, judge, and rewarder. He took the
scepter when it departed from Judah, and is exalted far
above all principality and power and might and dominion,
and has a name above every name, all executive power
in heaven and earth being given to him as Mediator.
Thus, as Mediator, the kingdom of heaven is his kingdom. He reigns not only as King of kings and Lord of
lords but seated on the throne of his father David, he is
forever King in Zion and is head over all things to his
church. His kingdom is not of this world, neither are
his subjects of this world, though some of them are in it.

He sent out his disciples to appear in a distinct character from the world and to be a light to it by imitating
his example and by exhibiting his spirit and temper.
They ought not to say, as the Jews did, that they have
no king but Cæsar, for they have an everlasting King
and kingdom and laws perfect and eternal. They should,
therefore, set their affections on things above and not
on things beneath.

While the kingdoms of this world exist, Christians must remain in captivity to them and must obey all their laws which are not contrary to the laws of the gospel; otherwise they cannot remain peaceful, harmless, and blameless in the midst of a wicked world before whom they must shine as lights.

Though the church is now in captivity, yet her redemption draweth nigh, for God will soon "overthrow the throne of kingdoms," and the thrones will be cast down and the princes of this world will come to naught. The stone which was cut out of the mountain without hands will dash them to pieces, as the potter's vessel is shivered, and will become a great mountain and fill the whole earth; then the kingdom and the dominion and the greatness of the kingdom under the whole heaven shall be given to the people of the saints of the most high God whose kingdom is an everlasting kingdom and of whose dominion there shall be no end.

Though God, by his decree, has ordained civil governments and established kingdoms, and will by his providence make them subservient to the good of his church and people, and notwithstanding it is the duty of Christians to be in subjection to them and pay tribute, yet it does not follow that their genius and laws may not often be contrary to the genius and laws of the gospel, and when they are so Christians must not obey them nor count their lives dear to themselves. It should be distinctly remembered that when Christians were exhorted and commanded to be obedient to civil rulers, they were under heathen, idolatrous, civil governments, and those civil governments were by no means congenial with the spirit and precepts of the gospel ; still Christians were commanded to be in subjection to them ; not, however, without limitation, for they utterly refused obedience in many instances and nobly suffered or died as martyrs.

Thus civil government may be an ordinance of God, may be subservient to the good of the church, may be an instrument in God's hands of executing his wrath, and Christians may be bound to obey magistrates in all things not contrary to the gospel; and yet it will not follow that Christians may consistently with the gospel take up the sword or do anything to countenance war.

If it be the duty of Christians to take the sword and enter the field of battle at the command of their civil rulers, then there could be no impropriety in having armies wholly made up of real Christians, especially since it is the duty of every man to become a Christian ; and as professing Christian nations are almost constantly fighting each other, it would be perfectly proper for hosts of pious saints to be daily engaged in shedding each other's blood. But how would it appear, how does it appear, for those who have drunk into the same peaceful and heavenly spirit, who are united together by the tender ties of the Redeemer's blood, who are all members of the same family, and who hope through divine grace to dwell together in everlasting love and blessedness, to be fighting one another here with relentless fury?

Let us contemplate the subject, in this point of view, a little further. Suppose an English and an American frigate in the time of war, both manned entirely with

real Christians, should meet in a neutral port. Ought
they not then to conduct towards each other as brethren
of one common Lord? As they are all members of the
same family and have all been redeemed by the same
blood, and sanctified by the same divine spirit, they
surely must have the most tender affection for each
other, and it would be highly proper for them to meet
together for Christian fellowship, worship, and communion. Suppose, then, that they occasionally go on
board each other's ships for religious worship; that
their chaplains lead in their devotions, using such peti-
tions as these — praying that they may be all of one
heart and one mind in the knowledge of Christ, knit
together in the bonds of Christian love; that they may
have much of the wisdom from above which is first
pure, then peaceable, gentle, easy to be entreated; that
they may do good to all as they have opportunity, especially to the household of faith; that they may be meek
and gentle as lambs and harmless as doves; that they
may be kind and forgiving and that, like their Divine
Master, they may return good for evil and have their
affections on things above and not on things beneath;
after which they unitedly partake of the symbols of
Christ's broken body and shed blood, and then part
with the tenderest tokens of Christian fellowship and
love. They leave the port and meet again at sea. It
now becomes their duty, on the principles of war, instead
of meeting as Christian brethren, to meet as raging
tigers and discharge the flaming engines of death on
each other; and in order to perform "their duty to
their God and country," they must exert all their power

and skill to destroy one another. The dreadful struggle and carnage must be continued by both parties as long as both can fight. When half of their crews are wallowing in their blood and expiring in agonies, a violent effort must be made by one or both to board the other and end the contest sword in hand. Those hands which recently saluted each other with Christian love now plunge the envenomed steel into their brethren's bosoms. At length one is vanquished and yields to the other. Those who remain alive after the conflict again unite in prayer and give thanks to God that he has given them courage and strength to fight so nobly, and that he has shielded their lives in the hour of battle. Thus they again resume their Christian fellowship and communion. This mutual fellowship, communion, and love are perfectly consistent with Christian character and are required by it. The conduct which has been supposed as enemies when fighting is also entirely consistent with the principles of war and with the character of warriors, and is such as would be highly applauded and admired by the world. But is it not obviously and perfectly absurd and perfectly incompatible with the principles of the gospel for Christians to act in this twofold character? If, however, it is the duty of Christians to obey the command of their rulers and engage in war, then it would be perfectly proper for what has been supposed to take place. Christians may one day surround the table of the Lord together, and the next kill and destroy each other.

The god of this world, not being yet chained down to hell, deceives the nations and gathers them together to battle; but the children of peace, the citizens of Zion, ought not to mingle with them or listen to the deceiver. They should take to themselves not carnal weapons but the whole armor of God, that they may be able to stand in an evil day and to quench all the fiery darts of Satan.

Objection thirteenth. To deny the right of the magistrate to call on his subjects to take the sword is to deny that he is an avenger to execute wrath, though the gospel expressly declares that he is.

Answer. This conclusion does not follow unless it is a fact that God cannot and does not actually make him the instrument of doing it, by his providence, without his command; for, as we have already observed, men may fulfill the decrees of God under his providence, without his command, and be very criminal in the deed. God raised up the king of Assyria and made him the rod of his anger, to chastise his people and to execute wrath upon the ungodly nations around. " Howbeit he meant not so, but it was in his heart to *cut off* nations not a few." And God declared, with reference to him, "that when he had performed his whole work he would punish the fruit of his stout heart and the glory of his high looks." It will not be contended that warlike nations are commanded by God to destroy and trample down the nations of the earth as the dust of their feet; yet, when they do so, they doubtless fulfill his high decree and are avengers to execute his wrath on a wicked world.

The beast represented in the Revelation with seven heads and ten horns has generally been considered as an emblem of nations. These ten horns, or powers, are

to hate the great harlot of Babylon; to eat her flesh
and burn her with fire; and though they destroy the
greatest enemy of the church, and in this way are ministers of good to her, yet they receive their power and
their seat and their authority from the old serpent, the
dragon. And a magistrate or king may be a minister
of good to the church and an avenger to execute wrath,
and still be very wicked in the deed and use very
unlawful means to accomplish the end. While he ful-
fills the decree of Heaven, he acts not in obedience to
the command of God, but to the dictates of his own
lusts and passions.

Objection fourteenth. The passages of Scripture which
have been quoted against retaliation and which inculcate love to enemies and the returning of good for evil
have reference to individuals in their conduct towards
each other, but have no relation to civil government and
are not intended as a rule of duty for one nation towards
another; they therefore have no bearing on the subject of war.

Answer. Those precepts of the gospel appear to be
binding universally without any limitation, and men
have no right to limit that which God has not limited.
If the commands of the gospel are binding upon every
one in his individual capacity, then they must be binding upon every one in any collective body, so that
whatever is morally wrong for every individual must
be equally wrong for a collective body; and a nation is
only a large number of individuals united so as to act
collectively as one person. Therefore, if it is criminal
for an individual to lie, steal, quarrel, and fight, it is also

criminal for nations to lie, steal, quarrel, and fight. If it is the duty of an individual to be kind and tender-hearted and to have a forgiving and merciful disposition, it is likewise the duty of nations to be kind, forgiving, and merciful. If it is the duty of an individual to return good for evil, then it is the duty of nations to return good for evil.

It is self-evident that individuals cannot delegate power to communities which they do not possess themselves. Therefore, if every individual is bound to obey the precepts of the gospel and cannot as an individual be released from the obligation, then individuals have no power to release any collective body from that obligation. To say that God has given to nations a right to return evil for evil is begging the question, for it does not appear and cannot be shown that God has restricted the precepts of the gospel to individuals, or that he has given any precepts to nations as such, or to any other community than his own covenant people or church. This objection makes government an abstraction according with the common saying, "Government is without a soul."

No practice has a more corrupt tendency than that of attempting to limit the Scriptures so as to make them trim with the corrupt practices of mankind. Whoever, for the sake of supporting war, attempts to limit these precepts of the gospel to individuals and denies that they are binding upon nations destroys one of the main pillars by which the lawfulness of war is upheld. The right of nations to defend themselves with the sword is argued on the supposed right of individual self-preservation ; as it is said to be right for individuals to defend themselves with deathly weapons, so it is lawful for nations to have recourse to the sword for defense of their rights. But if these passages are applicable to individuals and prohibit them from acts of retaliation, and if the rights of nations are founded on the rights of individuals, then nations have no right to retaliate injury.

Objection fifteenth. Christians, with comparatively few exceptions, have not doubted the lawfulness of war, and many have actually fought and bled on the field of battle and considered themselves in the way of their duty. And shall all our pious forefathers be condemned for engaging in war?

Answer. It is admitted that many pious people have engaged in war, but they might have been in an error on this subject as well as on many other subjects. Many of our pious forefathers engaged in the slavery of their fellow-men, and thought themselves in the way of their duty; but does it follow that they were not in an error? The circumstance that multitudes defend a sentiment is no certain evidence of its truth. Some of the reformers were objected to because the multitude were against them. Popularity, however, ever has influenced and ever will influence mankind more than plain gospel duty, until the earth shall be filled with the abundance of peace. But notwithstanding this, it is not right to follow the multitude to do evil. All ought to remember that they have no right to follow the example of any one any further than that example coincides with the example of Christ or the precepts of the gospel; all other standards are fallible and dangerous.

If real Christians have, from mistaken zeal, prayed against each other and fought each other and shed each other's blood, this does not justify war.

Objection sixteenth. If Christians generally should adopt these sentiments, it would be impossible for them to subsist in this world in its present state, and if they did continue it must be in abject slavery. They would become hewers of wood and drawers of water to the tyrannical and oppressive, and would only encourage them in their deeds of wickedness. The injustice of men must be restrained or the earth will again be filled with violence. The necessity of the case is such that mankind would be warranted to take up arms to maintain their rights and repel oppressors, if the Scriptures were silent on the subject.[1]

Answer. We have the history of the heathen world to teach us what mankind are without the light of revelation. They are full of all unrighteousness, covetousness, maliciousness ; full of enmity, murder, debate, deceit, malignity ; they are proud, boasters, without natural affection, implacable, unmerciful. Now the very design of the gospel is to subdue and overcome these abominable passions and dispositions ; not however by returning violence for violence but by producing virtues directly contrary. The great duty of Christians is to be a light to this wicked world by exhibiting in their conduct and conversation the spirit and temper of the gospel. If such were the practice of Christians, we have reason to believe that wicked men would be overawed and

[1] All these objections introduced are carefully selected from some of the ablest advocates for the lawfulness of war.

deterred from their violence in a great measure. Besides, if all real Christians should utterly refuse to bear arms for the destruction of their fellow-men, it would greatly diminish the strength and boldness of warlike nations, so that it would be impracticable for them to prosecute war with the vigor and fury that they now do.

But if the gospel prohibits war, then to urge the necessity of the case against the commands of God is open rebellion against his government as well as total distrust of his word and providence.

If Christians live in habitual obedience to God's commands, they have the promise that all things shall work together for their good, and they have no reason to fear them that kill the body and after that " have no more that they can do."

It is strange that Christians should have so great a reluctance to suffer inconvenience in worldly things for the sake of the gospel. The scoffs and persecutions of the world and the fear of the loss of worldly things are powerful barriers against *Christian* warfare. The gospel teaches us that all who live godly in Christ Jesus shall suffer persecution, and that through much tribulation the saints must enter into the kingdom of heaven; and is it not plainly owing wholly to their conformity to the world that they now suffer so little persecution and practice so little self-denial? If there is reserved for them an eternal weight of glory, what if they, like their Divine Master, should not have where to lay their heads? If they are to inherit a crown of immortal glory, what if they are called to suffer the loss of earthly things? If they are hereafter to reign as kings and priests unto God, what if they are not ranked among the great and honorable of the earth ? If they suffer with Christ, then will they also reign with him ; but if they deny him, he also will deny them ; and if they are ashamed of him, he will also be ashamed of them before his Father and the holy angels. Let Christians then obey his commands and trust to his protection while they resolutely abstain from the wicked practices of the world.

Objection seventeenth. It is the duty of mankind to use means for the preservation of life and liberty; they must till the ground, if they expect a crop. It would be presumptuous for them to pray for and to expect their daily bread without using such means as God has put in their power to obtain it; and it would be equally presumptuous to expect the preservation of their lives and liberties without using such means to preserve and defend them as God has put into their hand ; they must act as well as pray.

Answer. That using means is the duty of Christians, there can be no doubt ; but they must be such as God has appointed, and not such as human wisdom may dictate. There is no dispute as to the propriety of using means, but only as to the kind of means which Christians ought to use. The weapons of their warfare are not carnal, but spiritual, and they are mighty through God to the pulling down the strongholds of sin and Satan. It is often said, If you wish to put a stop to war, spread the gospel through the world. We would inquire, If the gospel tolerates war, how will its universal diffusion put a stop to war ?

As has already been observed, it would be open rebellion to do what God has forbidden, and high-handed presumption to ask his aid in the things which he has prohibited.

Objection eighteenth. Some ecclesiastical historians inform us that Christians in the early ages of the church, though they contended so firmly for the faith as to suffer martyrdom rather than submit to idolatry, yet did not refuse to bear arms in defense of their country, even when called upon by heathen magistrates, and their example ought to have weight with us.

Answer. The testimony of the early Fathers is entitled to regard, but must not be considered as infallible authority, for they were men of like passions with others and cannot be followed safely any farther than they followed Christ. But the weight of their testimony on the subject, I apprehend, will be found to stand directly against the lawfulness of war on Christian principles.

Erasmus, who was an eminent scholar, and who was probably as well acquainted with the sentiments of the primitive Fathers as any modern writer, in his *Antipolemos, or Plea against War*, replies to the advocates of war as follows : "They further object those opinions or decrees of the Fathers in which war seems to be approved. Of this sort there are some, but they are only late writers, who appeared when the true spirit of Christianity began to languish, and they are very few; while, on the other hand, there are innumerable ones among the writers of acknowledged sanctity which absolutely forbid war; and why should the few rather than the many intrude themselves into our mind?"

Barclay, who examined the writings of the Fathers on this subject, says, " It is as easy to obscure the sun at midday as to deny that the primitive Christians renounced all revenge and war."

Clarkson, who also examined the Fathers, declares that " every Christian writer of the second century who notices the subject makes it unlawful for Christians to bear arms."

Clarkson has made copious extracts from the writings of the Fathers against war, a few of which, as quoted by him and others, shall be inserted here.

Justin Martyr and Tatian both considered the devil the author of war.

Justin Martyr, while speaking of the prophecies relating to the days of peace, says, "That this prophecy is fulfilled you have good reason to believe, for we who in times past killed one another do not now fight with our enemies." Clarkson adds, "It is observable that the word 'fight' does not mean to strike, beat, or give a blow, but to fight in war ; and the word 'enemy' does not mean a common adversary who has injured us, but an enemy of state."

Irenæus says that Christians in his day " had changed their swords and their lances into instruments of peace, and that they knew not how to fight."

Maximilian and a number of others in the second century actually suffered martyrdom for refusing, on gospel principles, to bear arms.

Celsus made it one of his charges against the Christians that they refused to bear arms for the Emperor. Origen, in the following century, admitted the fact and justified the Christians on the ground of the unlawfulness of war itself.

Tertullian, in his discourse to Scapula, tells us "that no Christians were to be found in the Roman armies."

In his declaration on the worship of idols he says, "Though the soldiers came to John and received a certain form to be observed, and though the Centurion believed, yet Jesus Christ, by disarming Peter disarmed every soldier afterwards ; for custom can never sanction an illicit act."

Again, in his *Soldier's Garland*, he says : "Can a soldier's life be lawful, when Christ has pronounced that he who lives by the sword shall perish by the sword? Can one who professes the peaceable doctrine of the gospel be a soldier when it is his duty not so much as to go to law? And shall he who is not to avenge his own wrongs be instrumental in bringing others into chains, imprisonment, torment, and death ? "

He tells us, also, that the Christians in his day were sufficiently numerous to have defended themselves if their religion had permitted them to have recourse to the sword.

There are some marvelous accounts of Christian soldiers related by Eusebius ; but Valesius, in his annotations on these accounts, has abundantly proved them to be fabulous, though he was not opposed to war and could have had no other object but to support the truth. Eusebius, in his orations on Constantine, uses such extravagant adulation, which falls but little short of idolatry, that his account of Christian warriors ought to be received with great caution, especially when we recollect that church and state were, in his day, united.

On the whole, it is very evident that the early Christians did refuse to bear arms, and although one of their objections was the idolatrous rites connected with military service, yet they did object on account of the unlawfulness of war itself.

We have no good evidence of Christians being found in the armies until we have evidence of great corruption in the church. But admitting that we had good evidence that there were professing Christians in the army at an early period of the church, I apprehend it would be of little importance, for the idolatrous rites and ceremonies of the heathen armies were of such a nature as to be totally inconsistent with Christian character, and the example of idolatrous Christians surely ought to have no weight.

Some objections of less importance might be stated which have from time to time been made against the sentiments here advocated ; but to state and reply to everything that might be said is not necessary. Specious objections have been and still are made to almost every doctrine of Christianity. Mankind can generally find some plausible arguments to support whatever they wish to believe. The pleas in favor of war are very congenial with the natural feelings of the human heart, and unless men will examine with a serious, candid, and prayerful disposition to ascertain the truth as it is in Jesus, they will be very likely to imbibe and defend error.[1]

[1] The last point American Christians will give up is the justification of their fathers in the War of the Revolution.

The writer, though far from supposing that every-thing he has said on a subject that has been so little discussed is free from error, is conscious of having endeavored to examine it with seriousness and candor, and feels satisfied that the general sentiments he has advanced are according to godliness. He sincerely hopes that every one who may peruse these pages will do it in the meek and unbiased spirit of the gospel, and then judge whether war can be reconciled with the lamblike example of Christ; whether it is really for-giving the trespasses of enemies, loving and doing them good, and returning good for evil; for if it is not, it is unquestionably inconsistent with the spirit and the precepts of Christianity.

All who earnestly desire and look for the millennial glory of the church should consider that it can never arrive until the spirit and practice of war are abolished. All who love our Lord Jesus Christ in sincerity cannot but ardently desire that wars may cease to the ends of the earth and that mankind should embrace each other as brethren. If so, is it not their duty to do all in their power to promote so benevolent an object? Ought not every individual Christian to conduct in such a manner that if every other person imitated his example it would be best for the whole? If so, would they not immedi-ately renounce everything that leads to wars and fight-ings and embrace everything which would promote that glorious reign of righteousness and peace for which they earnestly hope, long, and pray? "The work of righteousness shall be peace, and the effect of right-eousnesss, quietness and assurance forever."

HYMN

SUGGESTED BY THE PRECEDING TRAIN OF THOUGHT, AND APPENDED
TO THE ORIGINAL EDITION OF THE ESSAY ON WAR

Great Sun of glory, rise and shine,
   Dispel the gloom of night ;
Let the foul spirits stretch their wings,
   And fly before thy light.

Rebuke the nations, stop their rage,
   Destroy the warrior's skill,
Hush all the tumults of the earth;
   O speak ! say, " Peace, be still."

Break, break the cruel warrior's sword,
   Asunder cut his bow,
Command him by thy sovereign word
   To let the captives go.

No more let heroes' glory sound,
   No more their triumphs tell,
Bring all the pride of nations down —
   Let war return to hell.

Then let thy blessed kingdom come,
   With all its heavenly train,
And pour thy peaceful spirit down,
   Like gentle showers of rain.

Then shall the prowling beasts of prey,
  Like lambs be meek and mild;
Vipers and asps shall harmless twine
  Around the weaned child.

The happy sons of Zion sit
  Secure beneath their vines;
Or, shadowed by their fig-tree's tops,
  Shall drink their cheering wines.

The nations to thy scepter bow,
  And own "thy gentle sway";
Then all the wandering tribes of men
  To thee their tribute pay.

Angelic hosts shall view the scene,
  Delighted, spread their wings;
Down to the earth again they fly,
  And strike their lofty strings.

The listening nations catch the sound,
  And join the heavenly choir,
To swell aloud the song of praise,
  And vie with sacred fire.

"Glory to God on high!" they sound,
  In strains of angels' mirth;
"Good will and peace" to men, they sing,
  Since heaven is brought to earth.

THE MEDIATOR'S KINGDOM NOT OF THIS WORLD: BUT SPIRITUAL

By an Inquirer

The writer of the following pages has, for a considerable time, doubted the propriety of some of the common practices of Christians. To satisfy himself he has, if he is not deceived, candidly and diligently examined the Scriptures with a view to ascertain and practice the truth. After considerable inquiry his doubts increased. He then applied to some highly respectable and pious friends, who frankly acknowledged that they had never fully examined the subject, as they had never had any doubt concerning it. They judged the matter weighty and advised him to arrange his thoughts and commit them to paper. This he has endeavored to do as well as a very infirm state of body and a press of commercial business would admit. After submitting what he had written to some of his friends, they unanimously advised him to lay it before the public, hoping that it might have a tendency to call the subject into notice and lead to a more complete and full examination. With this view he has ventured to commit the following sheets to the press. He has only to beg that the Christian who may take the trouble to read them will not be so solicitous to reply to the arguments as to examine and illustrate the truth.

The kingdom of our glorious Mediator is but little noticed in the world, yet it is precious in the eyes of the Lord. The Lord hath chosen Zion. She is the redeemed of the Lord. He hath said, he who touches her touches the apple of his eye. She is purchased by the blood of the Lamb, sanctified by the Spirit of grace, and defended by the arm of Omnipotence. Notwithstanding she may still be covered with sackcloth, the days of her mourning have an end. The Lord will raise her from the dust and make her an eternal excellency and the joy of many generations. The mystical body of Christ is composed of that innumerable company which no man can number, — out of every nation and kindred and people and tongue, — which will finally stand before the throne of God and the Lamb, clothed with white robes and palms in their hands. It is but one body, although composed of many members. The temple, which was a symbol of the church, was composed of many stones, although but one building. The spiritual temple is built of lively stones upon the foundation of the apostles and prophets, Jesus Christ himself being the chief corner stone. This spiritual temple will continue to rise under different dispensations until the elect are gathered together from the four winds of heaven and the top stone is carried up with shouts of Grace, Grace, unto it!

The Mediator's kingdom is not of this world. "Jesus answered, My kingdom is not of this world: if my kingdom were of this world, then would my servants fight, that I should not be delivered to the Jews" (John xviii. 36). In remarking upon these words we are naturally led to consider,

I. What the Mediator's kingdom is.

II. Its nature.

III. Its laws.

From which we propose to make several inferences and illustrations for improvement.

Agreeably to the arrangement of our subject, we shall first endeavor to ascertain what the kingdom of the Mediator is; or that kingdom which he so emphatically calls "My Kingdom," in distinction from all other kingdoms. "Jesus answered, My kingdom—" Our glorious Mediator takes to himself the majesty of a sovereign and claims a kingdom. In his mediatorial character he possesses, in an extensive sense, universal empire. He is exalted far above all principality and power and might and dominion, and has a name which is above every name. He is King of kings and Lord of lords. He is not only king on his holy hill of Zion but rules amongst the nations. He is, however, in an appropriate sense, king of saints under the gospel dispensation, as he governs the worlds with a view to his own glory and their exaltation.

That the church, under the gospel dispensation, is in a special manner the kingdom of heaven or the kingdom which Christ so often called his kingdom appears evident (it is thought) from many passages of Scripture. The prophet Daniel, while interpreting the symbols of the four great empires which were to arise in the earth, adds that "in the days of these kings shall the God of heaven set up a kingdom which shall never be destroyed." This kingdom could not be the Church Universal, for that was established in the family of Adam and had continued without being broken in a line of holy men down to the prophet's day. It must therefore have a special reference to something future. When John the Baptist came preaching, he said, "Repent ye, for the kingdom of heaven is at hand," fully implying that it had not

then commenced. He preached repentance preparatory
to ushering in that kingdom which the God of heaven
was about to set up. In the days of the fourth great
kingdom mentioned in the prophecy of Daniel the
Lord Jesus Christ came into our world to establish his
kingdom. As he entered upon his ministry he declared
that the time was fulfilled and that the kingdom of God
was at hand. When he first commissioned his disciples
and sent them forth to preach, he directed them to say
to their hearers, "The kingdom of God is come nigh
unto you." In speaking of John the Baptist, he says,
He was the greatest of prophets ; but adds, "He that
is least in the kingdom of God is greater than he";
which must be conclusive evidence that John the Baptist was not in the kingdom of God. At the Last Supper, after our Lord had blessed and partaken of the
bread, he said to his disciples, "I will not any more
eat thereof until it be fulfilled in the kingdom of God."
In like manner, after taking the cup, he said, "I will
not drink of the fruit of the vine until the kingdom of
God shall come." All of which seems fully to imply
that the kingdom which the God of heaven was about
to set up did not commence before the gospel dispensation. Christ came under the Mosaic dispensation,
that is, under the law, to redeem those who were under
the law, by the sacrifice of himself ; "and being found in
the fashion of a man, he humbled himself, and became
obedient unto death, even the death of the cross.
Wherefore God hath highly exalted him, and hath given
him a name which is above every name." After he
arose from the dead he appeared to his disciples "by

many infallible proofs, being seen of them forty days, and speaking of the things pertaining to the kingdom of God." "And Jesus came and spake unto them, saying, All power is given unto me in heaven and in earth. Go ye therefore, and teach all nations, baptizing them in the name of the Father, and of the Son, and of the Holy Ghost : teaching them to observe all things whatsoever I have commanded you : and, lo, I am with you always, even unto the end of the world. Amen." Here we see the Mediator possessing a kingdom and giving laws to his subjects and commanding obedience. Although his kingdom was then small, like a little leaven, yet it had the power to leaven the whole lump. The stone which was cut out of the mountain without hands will become a great mountain and fill the whole earth. Every knee must finally bow to his scepter and every tongue confess that he is Lord to the glory of God the Father.

From this concise view of the subject we conclude that the kingdom of God, or Christ's kingdom, is in a special manner the gospel dispensation which was not completely established until after the resurrection of our Lord.

II. The next point of inquiry is its nature. "Jesus answered, My kingdom is not of this world." By this we understand the Mediator's kingdom, not being of this world, supposes that its nature, its laws, and its government are all distinct from the nature, laws, and governments of this world. That the Mediator's kingdom is not of this world, but spiritual, heavenly, and divine, will fully appear, it is apprehended, from the following reasons.

1st. From the character of the King. He was not born like the kings of the earth. He was the Son of the living God and Heir of all things. He was conceived by the power of the Holy Ghost and born of a virgin. His birth was not celebrated with the earthly pomp of princes, but by a few humble shepherds and a choir of angels. His palace was a stable and his cradle a manger. When a child he was not amused with toys, but was about his Father's business. When he was dedicated to his ministry, it was not by the appointment of kings, or the consecration of bishops, but by the baptism of his humble forerunner, and the descent of the Holy Ghost in a bodily shape like a dove, and a voice from the excellent glory, saying, "This is my beloved Son, in whom I am well pleased." His companions were the despised fishermen of Galilee and the angels of heaven. He was "a man of sorrow and acquainted with grief"; yet he was the eternal Son of the eternal Father. Nature owned his voice and devils trembled at his power; but he was despised and rejected of men. When he fed the hungry multitude, they were gratified with the loaves and fishes and sought to make him a king; but he departed out of the place; for his kingdom was not of this world. When Satan, the god of this world, offered him all the kingdoms of this world and the glory of them if he would only fall down and worship him, he rebuked him with holy contempt and said, Get thee hence, Satan; for his kingdom was not of this world. The Mediator did not intermeddle with the affairs of the governments of this world; for his kingdom was not of this world. When he was solicited to command a brother to divide his earthly substance, instead of complying with the request he only gave a pointed admonition and said, "Man, who made me a judge, or a divider, over you?" When his enemies endeavored to catch him in his words by extorting from him something unfavorable to the laws of Cæsar, Jesus answered them and said, "Render to Cæsar the things which are Cæsar's, and to God the things which are God's." When they demanded of him tribute, and that unjustly, according to their own laws, he paid it without a murmur, to set an example of peace and quietness for his disciples. In all things he avoided interfering or meddling with the governments of this world.

2dly. From the representations of the Bible, "The kingdom of God is righteousness, peace, and joy in the Holy Ghost." The Mediator's kingdom is founded in right. His scepter is a right scepter. He rules in righteousness. "The unrighteous shall not inherit the kingdom of God." Righteousness is opposed to all injustice, oppression, and cruelty; it regards the rights of God and man; it requires love to the Lord our God with all our heart, with all our mind, and with all our strength, and to our neighbors as ourselves. His kingdom is a kingdom of peace; he is the Prince of Peace. At his birth the angels sang, "Peace on earth, and good will to men." Peace is opposed directly to all contention, war, and tumult, whether it regards individuals, societies, or nations. It forbids all wrath, clamor, and evil speaking. It forbids the resistance of evil or retaliation, and requires good for evil, blessing for cursing, and prayer for persecution. Our glorious Mediator not only exhibited a pattern of peace in his life but preached peace in the great congregation. His last and richest legacy to his disciples was the gift of peace: " My peace I leave with you, my peace I give unto you: not as the world giveth, give I unto you." Christ came in the power of the Spirit, and was full of the Holy Ghost. It is the communion of the Holy Ghost which fills the kingdom of heaven with that joy which is unspeakable and full of glory. " Except a man be born of the Spirit, he cannot enter into the kingdom of heaven." Finally, we have his own express declaration, " My kingdom is not of this world."

From what has been said it may be concluded that the Mediator's kingdom is, in a special sense, the gospel dispensation, or the kingdom of heaven, and that it is not of this world, but spiritual, heavenly, and divine. And this brings us to notice,

III. The laws by which it is governed. It is governed by the same laws which regulate the heavenly hosts. "Be ye therefore perfect, even as your Father in heaven is perfect," is the command of our Divine Master. It is the kingdom of heaven. " Jesus said, My kingdom is not of this world: if my kingdom were of this world, then would my servants fight, that I should not be delivered to the Jews." The laws of the Mediator's kingdom require supreme love to God. Jesus said, " Thou shalt love the Lord thy God with all thy heart, and with all thy soul, and with all thy mind; this is the first and great commandment." This implies right apprehension of his being and perfections, and supreme love to his word and delight in his law, such as the

sweet singer of Israel expressed: O how I love thy law!
it is my meditation day and night.   It implies unlimited
confidence in God and unshaken belief in the testimony
he has given of his Son and a spirit of filial obedience
to all his precepts.

The laws of the Mediator's kingdom require love to
man: "Thou shall love thy neighbour as thyself."
This prohibits rendering to any man evil for evil ; but,
contrariwise, it demands blessing.   It utterly forbids
wrath, hatred, malice, envy, pride, revenge, and fighting; but requires, on the contrary, meekness, forgiveness, long-suffering, tenderness, compassion, and mercy.
The subjects of the Mediator's kingdom are commanded
to do good to all as they have opportunity ; but especially to those of the household of faith.   This command extends not only to the gentle and kind but to
the disobedient and froward ; to friends and to enemies.
"If thine enemy hunger, feed him ; if he thirst, give
him drink," is the command of our Lord.   This injunction, it is apprehended, is directly opposed to resisting
the oppression of enemies by force.   Jesus said, "If
my kingdom were of this world, then would my servants fight"; but, instead of avenging wrongs, the
explicit direction is "to overcome evil with good."
The Mediator is the only avenger of the wrongs done
to his subjects: "For it is written, Vengeance is mine,
and I will repay, saith the Lord."   In a special manner
the subjects of the Mediator must love the brethren.
They must visit the widow, the fatherless, and the
afflicted, and live unspotted from the world.   The Lord
accepts every act of kindness done to the brethren as

done to himself, and regards every act of injustice, cruelty, and revenge towards them as expressed towards himself. He considers them his own property, the purchase of his blood. He will, therefore, not only be their portion but their defense ; a wall of fire round about them and a glory in the midst. The Mediator sits as King upon his holy hill of Zion, and is swaying his scepter in righteousness throughout his vast dominions.

Having very briefly considered what the Mediator's kingdom in a special manner is, its nature and its laws, we now pass, as was proposed, to make several inferences and illustrations.

1st. If the Mediator's kingdom is in a special manner the gospel dispensation, and its nature and laws are not of this world, but spiritual, heavenly, and divine, then we may infer that the kingdoms of this world are not united to the kingdom of our Lord, but are opposed to it. If they are not for him, they are against him ; and if they gather not with him, they scatter abroad. They must, therefore, be at war with the Lamb; but the Lamb shall overcome them, for he hath on his vesture and on his thigh a name written, King of kings and Lord of lords. The great conflict in our world is between the kingdom of the Mediator and the kingdom of Satan ; but the victory is not uncertain. Although the " heathen rage, and the people imagine a vain thing, the kings of the earth set themselves, and the rulers take counsel together, against the Lord, and against his Anointed, saying, Let us break their bands asunder, and cast away their cords from us. He that sitteth in the

heavens shall laugh : the Lord shall have them in deri-
sion. Then shall he speak to them in his wrath, and
vex them in his sore displeasure." "Out of his mouth
goeth a sharp sword, that with it he should smite the
nations; and he shall rule them with a rod of iron : and
he treadeth the winepress of the fierceness and wrath
of Almighty God."

The Psalmist, by the Holy Ghost, says of Christ,
"Thou shalt break them with a rod of iron; thou shalt
dash them to pieces like a potter's vessel." Again,
"He shall cut off the spirit of princes; he is terrible to
the kings of the earth." Isaiah, by the revealing spirit,
had the scenes of futurity opened to his view. He saw
the glorious Redeemer marching through the earth in
the greatness of his power ; for he saw, by prophetic
vision, the great day of his wrath appear, and none but
his redeemed were able to stand. In view of the dreadful scene his soul was filled with astonishment, and he
exclaims : "Who is this that cometh from Edom, with
dyed garments from Bozrah? this that is glorious in
his apparel, travelling in the greatness of his strength?
I that speak in righteousness, mighty to save. Wherefore art thou red in thine apparel, and thy garments
like him that treadeth in the winefat? I have trodden
the winepress alone ; and of the people there was none
with me : for I will tread them in my anger, and trample
them in my fury ; and their blood shall be sprinkled
upon my garments. For the day of vengeance is in my
heart, and the year of my redeemed is come. I looked,
and there was none to help ; and I wondered there was
none to uphold : therefore mine arm brought salvation

unto me; and my fury, it upheld me. And I will tread down the people in my anger, and make them drunk in my fury, and I will bring down their strength to the earth." From this it appears that the nations of the earth will be gathered like the grapes of a vineyard, and cast into the great wine press of the wrath of God Almighty; and the great Redeemer will thresh them in his anger and trample them in his fury. Their destruction must be inevitable if their laws and governments are directly opposed to the Mediator's kingdom. When he shall come out of his place to shake terribly the nations of the earth, then the *earth*[1] will no longer cover the blood of the slain; for he will make inquisition for blood, and write up the nations. Then he will stain the pride of all glory and bring into contempt all the honorable of the earth. The nations will be like stubble before the devouring fire, and will be chased away like chaff before the whirlwind, and no place will be found for them.

The interpretation of the symbols of the four great empires by the prophet Daniel fully confirms this idea. In first describing the vision to Nebuchadnezzar he says: "Thou sawest till that a stone was cut out without hands, which smote the image upon his feet that were of iron and clay, and brake them to pieces. Then was the iron, the clay, the brass, the silver, and the

---

[1] The earth, in symbolical language, is supposed by the writer to denote civilized nations, in distinction from uncivilized, which are symbolized by the agitated sea. Civilized nations will no longer cover the blood of the slain, under the specious idea of defending their rights and liberties.

gold, broken to pieces together, and became like the chaff of the summer threshingfloors; and the wind carried them away, that no place was found for them: and the stone that smote the image became a great mountain, and filled the whole earth." The prophet thus interprets the vision: "And in the days of these kings shall the God of heaven set up a kingdom, which shall never be destroyed: and the kingdom shall not be left to other people, but it shall break in pieces and consume all these kingdoms, and it shall stand for ever. Forasmuch as thou sawest that the stone was cut out of the mountain without hands, and that it brake in pieces the iron, the brass, the clay, the silver, and the gold; the great God hath made known to the king what shall come to pass hereafter."

Thus we see that the kingdoms of the world by not submitting to the kingdom of our Lord, but by making war with the Lamb, are devoted to awful destruction, for the Lamb will overcome them. His kingdom will stand, for it is an everlasting kingdom; and of his dominion there shall be no end. The gospel dispensation (or the kingdom of heaven) must remain forever, as it is governed by the same spirit which prevails in the eternal fountain of blessedness himself. It is therefore emphatically called the kingdom of God not only in distinction from the kingdoms of this world but in distinction from all the other dispensations of the church. It is not of this world; it is the kingdom of heaven, — the reign of righteousness, peace, and joy in the Holy Ghost.

2. If the Mediator's kingdom is not of this world, but spiritual, heavenly, and divine, and the kingdoms of

this world are opposed to it, then we may infer that the kingdoms of this world must belong to the kingdom of Satan. There are but two kingdoms in our world. At the head of one is the Mediator, and at the head of the other is Satan. Satan is the god of this world and reigns without a rival in the hearts of the children of disobedience. He is the prince of the power of the air. All the kingdoms of this world and the glory of them are given to him [1] until the time that God shall write up the nations and make inquisition for blood. Then the great battle of God Almighty will be fought, and the beast and the false prophet will be cast into a lake of fire ; and Satan will be bound a thousand years ; and the saints will take the kingdom and possess it ; and wars shall cease from under heaven. After the thousand years Satan will again be let loose, "and shall go out to deceive the nations which are in the four quarters of the earth, Gog and Magog, to gather them together to battle : the number of whom is as the sand of the sea." "And the devil who deceived them was cast into the lake of fire and brimstone, where the beast and the false prophet are, and shall be tormented day and night for ever and ever." Thus it appears that Satan is the mainspring of all warlike powers, and when he is bound wars will cease ; but as soon as he is again let loose they will rage. The writer is sensible that this will be a very unpopular doctrine with the men of this world, and with those worldly Christians

[1] If the kingdoms of this world do not belong to Satan, then it was no temptation to our Lord when he offered them to him. It is expressly said that he was " tempted of Satan."

who are struggling and teasing and panting for the profits and the honors of this world. If it is a fact that the nature and laws of the Mediator's kingdom are diametrically opposite to the kingdoms of this world, then the inference is irresistible that the kingdoms of this world belong not to the kingdom of our Lord but to the kingdom of Satan; and however unsavory the truth may be, it ought not to be disguised. Satan is the strong man, but the Mediator is the stronger, and he will bind him and spoil his goods. The Son of God was manifested that he might destroy the works of the devil. When he shall destroy the rage of the nations and the tumult of the people, then Satan's goods will be spoiled. When Satan is cast into the bottomless pit, tumult and war will retire with him back to hell; and instead of the blast of the trumpet and the groans of the dying will be heard the shouts of the saints and the songs of the redeemed. Then will be "heard as it were the voice of a great multitude, and as the voice of many waters, and as the voice of mighty thunderings, saying, Alleluia, for the Lord God Omnipotent reigneth."

3. If the Mediator's kingdom is not of this world, and the kingdoms of this world are under Satan's dominion, then we may infer the great impropriety of the subjects of the Mediator's kingdom using the weapons of this world and engaging in tumults, wars, and fightings. "Jesus answered, My kingdom is not of this world: if my kingdom were of this world, then would my servants fight, that I should not be delivered to the Jews." The Jews expected in their Messiah a

temporal prince; but because his kingdom was not of this world they crucified the Lord of life and glory. Had he only appeared in the pomp of this world and in the splendor of a temporal conqueror to vanquish the Romans who were in possession of their earthly Canaan and oppressing their nation, they would immediately have rallied round his standard and followed him to earthly conquest and glory. He was apparently too inattentive to their rights .and liberties (which the patriots of this world now emphatically call their dearest interests). They said, "If we let him alone, all men will believe on him; and the Romans shall take away both our place and our nation." It may be asked, Why were the Jews apprehensive, if all men should believe on him, the Romans would take away both their place and their nation? The answer does not appear difficult. They doubtless perceived that both his life and precepts directly opposed rendering vengeance to their enemies; and, on the contrary, demanded nothing less than love to their enemies, good for evil, and blessing for cursing. This they could not endure, as it directly opposed their carnal desires and filled them with malice against the Prince of Peace. They might, with much greater propriety than any nation under the gospel light, have said, "Shall we imbibe this pusillanimous spirit of doing good to those who oppress us and tamely bend our necks to the yoke of tyranny and suffer our dearest interests to be wrested from us without once making a struggle to defend them? Rather, let us arise and fight manfully, and defend our liberties or· die gloriously in their vindication." We say they might, with much greater propriety, have made these declarations than any under the light of the gospel, because they considered themselves under the Mosaic dispensation which had fully tolerated them not only in defensive but offensive war. But when they perceived that the doctrines of the Mediator were calculated to disannul their dispensation and extinguish their carnal hopes (notwithstanding his credentials were divine), their malice was kindled against him, and their vengeance was not satiated until they wreaked their hands in the blood of the Son of God. And we may confidently expect that wherever the same Spirit of Christ lifts up a standard against the same carnal policy and temporal interest there will follow the same spirit of envy, persecution, and revenge which was manifested against the Lord of life and glory. If any man (no matter who) will live godly in Christ Jesus, he shall suffer persecution. The Spirit of Christ is the same now that it was then, and the world is the same, the carnal heart is the same, and the great adversary of souls is the same. Only let it be styled "patriotic" to persecute the followers of the Lamb of God, and we should soon see the heroes of this world drunk with the blood of the martyrs of Jesus; and probably many would be as conscientious as Paul was while breathing out threatenings and slaughter against the disciples of the meek and lowly Jesus. It is not impossible that when the witnesses [1] are slain, their crime may be a

---

[1] The writer has for a length of time been of opinion that no event has ever yet happened to the church which answers to slaying the witnesses. It has been given as a reason by some that the witnesses

refusal to use carnal weapons in defense of their country.

As it is a matter of great practical consequence to know whether the subjects of the Prince of Peace are authorized in any case under the gospel dispensation to use carnal weapons or not, we propose in this inference to be a little more particular. Although it is supposed that the Lord Jesus Christ acted in a threefold capacity,—as God, Man, and Mediator,—yet we have never heard it questioned by Christians that all his conduct as man was to remain a perfect example for his brethren, and all his precepts a perfect rule for their duty. As his kingdom was not of this world, he did not intermeddle with the governments of this world; he only submitted to all their laws which were not contrary to the laws of his heavenly Father. He was meek and lowly; so little did he possess of this world that he had not where to lay his head. He went about continually doing good. He was full of compassion even to his enemies. He wept over Jerusalem. He was finally "brought as a lamb to the slaughter, and as sheep before their shearers are dumb, so he opened not his mouth."

have been slain, that so much light has been diffused since the art of printing was discovered, and since the Reformation, that no reason can ever again be found sufficiently plausible to satisfy the consciences of mankind in again taking the lives of their fellow-men in matters of conscience. If our country was invaded and a law should be passed that every man capable of bearing arms should equip himself for its defense, on penalty of being considered as an enemy and to be publicly executed accordingly in case of refusal for conscience' sake, there would not probably be wanting patriots sufficient to execute the laws; if they could not be found in our land of liberty, they might be found amongst the tyrants of the Old World.

When he was reviled he reviled not again, but committed himself to him who judges righteously. He prayed for his murderers and apologized for his persecutors, saying, "Father, forgive them, for they know not what they do." As the church under a former dispensation had divine authority for engaging in war, it is important to ascertain whether this authority was abrogated under the gospel dispensation or not.[1] That many things have been tolerated under one dispensation of the church and prohibited under another, most Christians allow. That the preceptive will of God is to be our only rule of duty, few Christians deny. The knowledge communicated to us of the preceptive will of God to his church, under the first dispensation, is very limited. We find, however, no authority for taking the life of man in any case, not even for

[1] If the permission given to the church under the Mosaic dispensation to engage in war has not been disannulled by the gospel dispensation (which is by no means granted), it is thought that it does not admit of the consequences which are generally drawn. The Israelites were God's covenant people and were utterly prohibited from making any covenant with the nations around them, or engaging with them in their wars. It must therefore be totally improper for God's covenant people now to unite with those who are strangers to the covenant of promise, and engage with them in their tumult and fightings. It is presumed that no one who has ever read our Constitution will pretend that the American nation has, in the Scriptural sense, made a covenant with God. If the analogy holds good in one point, it must in another; and in that case there is no alternative left for God's covenant people but either to withdraw from those who are not in covenant with God, or adopt a national religion which must be defended by the weapons of the nation. It is believed that those who will not admit that the permission granted to the Israelites to engage in war was abrogated by the gospel dispensation can never fully answer the arguments in favor of a national religion,

murder; but, on the contrary, a sevenfold vengeance was pronounced upon him who should slay the murderer. Under the patriarchal dispensation he that shed man's blood by man was his blood to be shed. In this, defensive war was tolerated. Under the Mosaic dispensation, not only defensive but offensive war was tolerated, and not only *war* was permitted, but *retaliation*, as, "an eye for an eye"; "a tooth for a tooth"; "life for life," etc.

The question to be decided is whether these regulations are still in force, or whether they were disannulled by the gospel dispensation? The life and precepts of our Lord and his disciples while under the unerring guidance of his spirit must be our only authority in this inquiry. That many things were done away by the gospel dispensation, none will deny who believe the gospel. The ceremonial part, which was only a shadow of good things to come, vanished away when the substance appeared; and not only the ceremonial part was abolished, but many other practices. Polygamy was permitted under the law, but forbidden under the gospel. Divorce was allowed under the Mosaic but prohibited under the gospel dispensation, except in the case of adultery. Under the Mosaic dispensation the penalty for whoredom was stoning to death. This penalty was not enforced under the gospel dispensation, as may be seen in John viii. 11. That all kinds of war, revenge, and fighting were utterly prohibited under the gospel dispensation we think appears evident not only from the life of our glorious Mediator but from his express precepts. "Jesus answered, My kingdom is

not of this world: if my kingdom were of this world,
then would my servants fight, that I should not be
delivered to the Jews." No comment can add force to
this passage, for it is apprehended that no language
can be more explicit against defensive war.

In Christ's Sermon on the Mount he quoted a passage from Exodus, "Ye have heard that it hath been
said, An eye for an eye, and a tooth for a tooth : but I
say unto you, That *ye resist not evil:* but whatsoever
shall smite thee on thy right cheek, turn to him the
other also." The force of this passage has generally
been obviated by saying that we are not to take all the
words of our Lord literally. Although this is admitted,
yet we are absolutely bound to take the spirit of every
word, if we can understand them, by comparing the
Scriptures with the Scriptures. That the spirit of this
passage is directly opposed to the one our Lord quoted
from Exodus, we think cannot fairly be denied ; and, of
course, it disannulled it, for he who had power to make
laws under one dispensation had power to abrogate
them under another.

The blessed Mediator did, in the most explicit manner, command his subjects to love their enemies and
render good for evil. This command we are of opinion
is totally incompatible with resisting them with carnal
weapons. He says, "But I say unto you which hear,
Love your enemies, do good to them which hate
you, and pray for them which despitefully use you."
Let us for one moment compare this precept with
defensive war and see if it can consistently be put
into practice. Suppose our country is invaded and a

professed disciple of the Prince of Peace buckles on the harness and takes the field to repel by the point of the sword his enemy. He advances amidst the lamentations of the wounded and the shrieks of the dying to meet his foe in arms. He sees his wrath kindled and his spear uplifted, and in this trying moment he hears his Lord say, "Love your enemy and render to him good for evil"; and his kindness to him is like Joab's to Amasa; he thrusts him through the heart and hurries him to the awful tribunal of his Judge, probably unprepared. Dear brethren, be not deceived; for God is not mocked. Who amongst our fellow-men would receive the thrust of a sword as an act of kindness? Only let conscience do its office, and there will be no difficulty in deciding whether defensive war is inconsistent with the gospel dispensation or not. Carnal and spiritual weapons will no more unite under the gospel dispensation than iron and miry clay.

Our very salvation depends on being possessed of a spirit of forgiveness to enemies. "If ye forgive not men their trespasses, neither will your Father forgive your trespasses." If men invade our rights and trespass upon our privileges, is it forgiveness to repel them at the point of the bayonet? The honest Christian will find no difficulty in conscientiously deciding this question, notwithstanding he may be slow of heart in believing all that is written.

All the conduct of our Lord had meaning to it, and much of it was with an express view to teach his disciples by way of example. A little before he was betrayed, he ordered his disciples to take swords. The object of this must have been either to use them for defense, or for some other purpose. The event proves that they were not taken for self-defense. The question then is, For what were they taken? The event appears fully to answer the question, viz.: To prohibit, by way of example, the use of them for self-defense in the most trying situation possible. If any situation would justify self-defense with carnal weapons, it must have been the situation in which our Lord and his disciples were placed at the time he was betrayed. They were in a public garden, and they were assaulted by a mob, contrary to the statutes of the Romans and the laws of the Jews; and the object was to take his life. This the disciples knew, and Peter judged it a proper time for defense, and drew his sword and smote a servant of the High Priest and cut off his ear. As our Lord's kingdom was not of this world, he would not suffer his subjects to use the weapons of this world in any situation. He therefore healed the wound they made and rebuked Peter for his mistaken zeal. "Then said Jesus unto him, Put up again thy sword into his place: for all they that take the sword shall perish with the sword. Thinkest thou that I cannot pray to my Father, and he would presently send me more than twelve legions of angels?" Here we see that our Lord not only forbade his disciples to use the sword in self-defense, but added a dreadful penalty to transgressors, — "all they that take the sword shall perish with the sword." The disciples did not then fully understand that his kingdom was not of this world.

As soon as they were prohibited using the weapons of this world they all forsook him and fled.[1]

The apostle James, in his epistle to the twelve tribes of Israel which were scattered abroad, asks them this

[1] Four things are noticeable from this history. *First*, That the subjects of the Mediator's kingdom have no right to use carnal weapons for defense, in the most trying situation possible. *Secondly*, The promulgation of a decree of heaven ; that all they (whether states, churches, or kingdoms) who take the sword shall perish with the sword. Every political or ecclesiastical body which is defended with the sword will by the sword be destroyed. In confirmation of this sentiment, we see while the great destroying powers were represented to St. John in the symbols of ferocious beasts, it was added, " If any man have an ear to hear, let him hear. He that leadeth into captivity shall go into captivity : he that killeth with the sword must be killed with the sword "; but in opposition to this it is said, " Here is the faith and the patience of the saints." We would inquire how the faith and the patience of the saints appear, if they, like the nations of the earth, lead into captivity and kill with the sword ? *Thirdly*, The weapon which the subjects of the Redeemer are to use for defense is here brought into view, viz., Prayer. Nothing which appears prevented our Lord from using this weapon when he was betrayed, but the necessity of the Scriptures being fulfilled. Had he prayed to his Father, more than twelve legions of ministering spirits would have appeared swift as lightning to discharge his will. At the time he shall come in all the glory of his Father the holy angels will be with him. He will break through the heavens in flaming fire and descend with the shout of the Archangel and the trump of God, and cleave asunder the earth beneath; and send forth his angels who will awake the sleeping millions from their tombs and gather together his elect and take them up into the air to be ever with their Lord. *Fourthly*, We may expect that angels will be sent to deliver the saints in the times of trouble. Angels are ministering spirits and are sent forth to minister to those who shall be the heirs of salvation. What a consolation it is that the subjects of the Mediator can apply for help in times of trouble to him who has the hosts of heaven at his command; and who has said he will never leave nor forsake them ! The angel of the Lord encampeth round about them who fear him, to deliver them out of all their trouble. If God be for them, who can be against them ?

question : " From whence come wars and fighting among you? come they not even of your lusts that war in your members? Ye lust, and have not: ye kill, and desire to have, and cannot obtain : ye fight and war, and yet ye have not." " Ye adulterers and adulteresses, know ye not that the friendship of the world is enmity with God? whosoever therefore will be a friend to the world is an enemy of God." From this we think it evidently appears that the warlike spirit of the world is directly opposed to God. The God of this world works effectually in the hearts of the children of disobedience and stirs up their lusts which war in their members and hurries them on to acts of cruelty, revenge, and fighting.

This subject is of so much practical consequence that it requires a few observations in reply to some of the arguments of worldly and unenlightened Christians in favor of using carnal weapons. It is said that government is an ordinance of God which exists throughout his vast dominion. In heaven above there are angels and archangels; and upon earth there are magistrates and powers; and in hell there is the prince of devils. That God in his holy providence has so disposed of events that governments of some kind or other do exist in all parts of his dominion, none but skeptics will deny. But who would pretend that the governments in heaven and hell are not diametrically opposite? One is the spirit of peace and love, and the other, rebellion and war. Perhaps the manifestation of these different spirits here on earth may fairly be the dividing line amongst its inhabitants, and show to which kingdom they belong.

They say all powers are ordained of God. Thus far they are correct, but it is apprehended that they do not make a proper distinction between the ordination of God and his preceptive will for man. So far as the former agrees with the latter, it is a rule of duty and cannot be any further. One is the rule of God's own procedure (if the expression is proper), and the other the rule of action for his creatures; but the counsel of God and his laws for man are often diametrically opposite. It is not improbable that this is part of the mystery of God which will, by and by, be finished.

The Lord Jesus Christ was delivered by the determinate counsel and foreknowledge of God; and yet, by wicked hands, he was crucified and slain. Here, as in the case of Pharaoh, and many other instances recorded, the divine counsel and the duty of man were directly opposite. To ascertain our duty we must look at the preceptive will of God and not to his eternal counsel. Although all powers are ordained of God, yet it must not be inferred that all the laws of the heathen or civilized world are to be a rule of duty for the Mediator's subjects, or that their spirit is agreeable to the spirit of the gospel dispensation. It is said, We are commanded to obey magistrates and every ordinance of man for the Lord's sake. All this is admitted. But these injunctions are either limited by other precepts or they are unlimited. If they are unlimited, then all who have died martyrs fell a sacrifice to superstition instead of duty. Notwithstanding these directions were intended as a rule for Christians in all ages, yet they were promulgated while the disciples were under idolatrous governments, and were never intended to encourage them to worship idols.

These commands must, therefore, be limited. The question is, How are they limited? We apprehend, by the spirit and other precepts of the gospel. We have already shown, we trust, that these absolutely prohibit war in every form. If so, then none of these injunctions can counteract the position we are examining. They only enjoin strict obedience to all human laws under which we live that do not contradict the spirit or precepts of the gospel; when they do, they are not binding and must be resisted; not, however, with carnal but spiritual weapons; we must take joyfully the spoiling of our goods and count not our lives dear unto ourselves.

It has been often said that he who refuses to comply with the commands of tne magistrate resists the powers that be, and, according to the apostle's reasoning, resists the ordinance of God and will receive to himself damnation. And, further, as all powers are the ordinance of God they ought to be supported, and if they cannot without, they must be even at the point of, the sword. Here the subject of the Mediator must make a distinction between resisting the "powers that be" by force of arms and refusing to obey their unlawful commands. It is not supposed that in one case he would obey and that in the other he would disobey the commands of his Master. No martyr ever considered himself as violating this precept in refusing to sacrifice to an idol at the command of an earthly power; neither will any subject of the Mediator view himself as violating it by refusing to use carnal weapons while he believes that his Lord

has utterly forbidden his using them. It is apprehended that if this proves anything upon the principles
of war, that it will prove too much for its advocates.
The command is to obey the powers that be and not
the powers that ought to be. If it is taken in an unlimited sense, it must prohibit resisting even tyrannical
powers, and would, of course, condemn every Christian
who engaged in the American Revolution. To say that
all power is in the hands of the people, and, of course,
it is the people who are the powers that be, is thought
to be but a quibble. We will suppose a very possible
case, — that a foreign power completely overturns the
government of the people and disannuls their laws and
gives a new code ; in that case, the command to obey
the powers that be would not be annihilated. The precept originally was given while the disciples were in
the midst of tyrannical governments. It is thought
that it is so far from tolerating defensive war that it is
opposed to it. The precepts of the gospel cannot be
dependent upon the convulsions of the nations. If
Christians are bound to aid with carnal weapons in
suppressing a rebellion, then, if the opposing power
gains the predominance, they must turn directly about
and fight the very power they were before supporting.
Such conduct would not become the citizens of Zion.
If it is said the powers that be are Christian rulers,
then we say, let them govern only by the laws of the
Mediator's kingdom, and we will bow with reverence
before them, and not teach for commandments the
doctrines of men, as we cannot receive human laws
for divine precepts.

It is stated that our Lord paid tribute, and that we are commanded to pay tribute to whom tribute is due, and that tribute supports the governments of this world. This is granted; but the Mediator's subjects are required also to lead peaceable and quiet lives; this is more promoted by paying tribute than by the refusal. Our Lord directs Peter to pay the tribute lest they should give offense. But paying tribute for the sake of preserving peace is a very different thing from actually engaging in war.

Whenever the Christian is called upon to pay money by way of taxes or tribute, he does not part with any spiritual treasure, but only earthly property, for which he has the example and precepts of the Lord. The currency of the world generally bears the ensign of the nation which made it. If it bears the image and super-scription of Cæsar, then "render to Cæsar the things that are Cæsar's, and unto God the things which are God's." Christians, however, whose hearts are upon this idol, will sooner give up their lives than their God. "The love of money is the root of all evil." The real Christian's treasure is in heaven and beyond the reach of the powers of earth or hell. The things of this world are but privileges loaned him, to be resigned at the call of his Lord. Shall he then fear those who can only kill the body and afterwards have no more that they can do? Rather, let him fear him who has power to destroy both soul and body in hell forever. It is better for him to suffer wrong than to do wrong.

The permission granted to the Jewish church to wage war has often been pleaded as authority for

Christians. If this proves anything, it proves too much, for not only defensive but offensive war was permitted under the Mosaic dispensation. This the tyrants of the world have not generally contended was right since the gospel dispensation. We think, however, that we have fully shown that this was abrogated under the gospel dispensation, and that all kinds of war were prohibited ; if so, it has no weight on the subject.[1]

It has been said that Christians with a small exception have never questioned the propriety of defensive war. As it regards nominal Christians, this statement is perhaps correct, but as it respects the real disciples of the Mediator, it is to be questioned. We hear of no Christians in the first ages of the church engaged in carnal warfare until we hear of great corruptions in the church. Most Protestants have been of opinion that those precious disciples who inhabited the dark valleys of Piedmont during the great corruptions of the nominal church were the Redeemer's true subjects. These disciples, of whom the world was not worthy, utterly

---

[1] Although it is not expected that any intelligent and candid Christian will attempt to say that the arguments which have been advanced may fairly apply to offensive but not to defensive war, yet some weak and unenlightened Christians may make the assertion. In answer to such we would observe that this would be begging the question and taking for granted the very subject in dispute. We cannot be satisfied with anything short of a candid answer, drawn directly from the spirit and precepts of the gospel. When it is fairly proved that under the gospel dispensation our Lord did draw a clear line of distinction between offensive and defensive war, and that he intended all such precepts as have been adduced to apply to the former and not to the latter, then we will acknowledge the weight of the argument. Until this is done we shall not consider our arguments as answered.

refused to engage even in defensive war, notwithstanding they were hunted down by their bloody persecutors.[1]

It has been often said that the Reformers, who were good men, did not hesitate to engage in defensive war, and that the Reformation was finally supported by the sword. That the Reformers were generally pious men is readily admitted, and that the Reformation, under divine providence, was a glorious event to the church is also granted. But the history of the Reformers, when written by their friends, abundantly manifests that they were men, subject to like passions with other men, and that all the means they employed could not be justified, either by the spirit or the precepts of the gospel.

Henry the Eighth was a vile man, but he was very active in protesting against the Pope because his holiness would not grant him a divorce. God makes the wrath of man praise him. It will not probably be a great length of time (in the opinion of the writer) before those churches which were defended with the sword will be destroyed by the sword.

---

[1] The writer perceives that he has made too unlimited a statement respecting the disciples who inhabited the valleys of Piedmont. Historians have generally considered those who dissented from the church of Rome during the dark ages as possessing similar sentiments. It is true they did agree in renouncing the authority of the Pope, but in other things they did not all agree. Some courted the protection of earthly powers and united with them in defending their rights by the point of the sword, and were finally destroyed by the sword. Others, instead of defending themselves with carnal weapons, fled from the face of the serpent and were, under divine providence, the seed of the church in the wilderness. It is the latter class to which the writer would be understood as referring.

It has been further urged that not only the Reformers but most pious Protestants have prayed for the prosperity of the arms of their country, and many have actually fought in the field of battle. All this is likewise admitted. But many pious men have had a mistaken zeal. It is fully believed that Protestants, generally, have been in the habit of considering the Reformation so glorious an event that they have very little inquired whether the means by which it was finally defended were agreeable to the spirit of the gospel or not. They have been taught from their earliest years to consider that the weapons of warfare used by the Reformers were lawful, so that they have not hesitated to follow their example. That the example and prayers of pious people ought to have weight is readily granted, but to place a blind confidence in them, we apprehend, is criminal, for their example is to be imitated no further than it agrees with the spirit and precepts of the gospel. These must forever remain a perfect standard of duty; whereas the practice of real Christians, owing to their imperfect state, is constantly changing and often contradictory. During the American Revolution, doubtless, real Christians were praying and fighting for the success of the American arms, and real Christians in the British service were praying and fighting for the success of his Majesty's arms. The truth is, they ought not to pray for war in any shape, but to pray that wars may cease from under heaven, and that God's kingdom may come and his will be done on earth as it is done in heaven; and not only to pray, but endeavor to advance the kingdom of heaven and put a stop to wars and bloodshed.   The opinions of pious people often vary with the increase of light which shines upon the church. One century ago most pious people believed in the propriety of the slave trade, but very few can now be found to advocate the abominable practice.   The nature of the crime has not changed, nor the evidence against it, but the truth is, that the opinion of pious people has materially changed upon this subject.   We ought always to remember that the example of pious people is to be of no weight any further than it agrees with the example of our Lord.   It is always unsafe to be looking too much to the fallible example of those whom we have esteemed pious for a rule of duty, while we have the unerring word in our hands to light our way; when any one is depending upon the example of Christians not under the immediate influence of divine inspiration for evidence to support his hypothesis, it is strong presumptive evidence that he has not the word of God in his favor.   By the word of God and by that *only* ought every controversy to be tried.

It is further urged that we are commanded to pray for kings and all in authority; it is true we must pray not only for kings but all men, even enemies.   This, however, does by no means imply that we are commanded to pray for a blessing upon their unhallowed undertakings; but it only implies that we must pray that they may be translated out of nature's darkness into the light of the gospel, and from the power of Satan unto the living God.

The great difficulty with the subjects of the Mediator ever has been, and still is, a want of faith in the

promises of God. They are prone to be afraid of consequences. They look nearly as much at consequences
as the children of Israel did while journeying from
Egypt to Canaan. The truth is, they ought to have
nothing to do with consequences, but only duties.
" Thus saith the Lord," should be their warrant and
only guide. If they implicitly follow the command, consequences are all safe in God's hand. Had Abraham
looked only at consequences, it is not probable he would
ever have been styled the Father of the Faithful. It is
not uncommon for timid and worldly Christians to be
alarmed at consequences and to argue in this manner :
they say, " Shall we stand still and suffer an assassin
to enter our houses and take our lives and property
without ever attempting to resist him ? " All this must
go upon the supposition that he who has said he will
never leave nor forsake his people, and is a very present
help in every time of need, will take no care of them.
No assassin could stand a moment before the prayer of
faith which would enter the heavens and reach the ears
of the Lord of Sabaoth. If faithless Christians cannot
be persuaded to look at the precepts and the promises,
but only at consequences, they ought, at least, to examine them well. Suppose God, in his holy providence,
should permit an assassin to take the life of one of his
dear children ; the consequence would be, he would
immediately be translated to glory; and possibly the
assassin might become a penitent ; but should he take
the life of the assassin in defending himself, the consequence then would be, he would hurry him into the
abyss of the damned where his probation would be

eternally ended. He who puts his trust in the Lord shall not fear what man can do to him; he will be like Mount Zion which cannot be moved.

Remember, dear brethren, that the weapons of our warfare are not carnal but spiritual, and mighty through God. "Finally, my brethren, be strong in the Lord, and in the power of his might. Put on the whole armour of God, that ye may be able to stand against the wiles of the devil. For we wrestle not against flesh and blood, but against principalities, against powers, against the rulers of the darkness of this world, against spiritual wickedness in high places. Wherefore take unto you the whole armour of God (here is the equipment of a soldier of Jesus Christ), that ye may be able to withstand in an evil day, and having done all, to stand. Stand therefore, having your loins girt about with truth, and having on the breastplate of righteousness; and your feet shod with the preparation of the gospel of peace; above all, taking the shield of faith, wherewith ye shall be able to quench all the fiery darts of the wicked. And take the helmet of salvation, and the sword of the Spirit, which is the word of God: praying always with all prayer and supplication in the Spirit, and watching thereunto with all perseverance and supplication for all saints." And the very God of peace shall be with you, and he will shortly bruise Satan under your feet. For yet a little while and the Almighty angel will come down with a great chain in his hand; and he will lay hold on the dragon, that old serpent, which is the devil and Satan, and will bind him a thousand years, and cast him into the bottomless pit, and shut him up, and set a seal upon him, that he shall deceive the nations no more until the thousand years are fulfilled. Then wars will cease from under heaven and the implements of death will be converted into the harmless utensils of husbandry, and there will be nothing to hurt nor destroy in all God's holy mountain. The stone which was cut out of the mountain without hands will become a great mountain and fill the whole earth. Then will be heard "a loud voice saying in heaven, Now is come salvation, and strength, and the kingdom of God, and the power of his Christ : for the accuser of our brethren is cast down, which accused them before God day and night. And they overcame him by the blood of the Lamb, and by the word of their testimony ; and they loved not their lives unto the death. Therefore rejoice, ye heavens, and ye that dwell in them."

It is, however, very important, dear brethren, that we keep it constantly in mind that the nature and precepts of the gospel are the same now as they will be then, in that glorious reign of righteousness and peace, and that it is our duty constantly to be influenced by the same spirit now which will then be manifested by the followers of the Lamb. The little leaven is of the same nature with whole lump when it is leavened. Let us therefore gird up the loins of our mind and watch unto prayer.

4. If the Mediator's kingdom is not of this world, but spiritual, heavenly, and divine, and if the kingdoms of this world are under the dominion of Satan, and if the subjects of Christ's kingdom are not permitted to

use carnal weapons, then we may infer who is the "great whore that sitteth upon many waters; with whom the kings of the earth have committed fornication, and the inhabitants of the earth have been made drunk with the wine of her fornication." A virgin or chaste woman is a familiar symbol in the Scriptures of the true church of God ; and an unchaste woman is as familiar a symbol of an apostate or corrupt church. As a lewd woman calls herself by the name of her husband, notwithstanding she has constant intercourse with other men, so the corrupt church calls herself by the name of Christ, notwithstanding she has constant illicit intercourse with the kings of the earth.[1] To understand the true nature of spiritual whoredom will assist us in ascertaining the bounds of mystical Babylon.

[1] As the writer has been for some time studying the symbolical language of the Scriptures, and intends (if the Lord will, unless some person more able should attempt an explanation) to give his views to the public, he will not be so particular at present in explaining the symbol of the great whore which sitteth upon many waters, as he otherwise should. He early perceived that the heavens and the earth, with all their furniture, were used as an alphabet, in the language of things, to represent moral subjects. His object has been to learn the true meaning of each symbol by comparing Scripture with Scripture. No language can be read until the alphabet is first learned. Symbolical language does not, like other languages, change with time and place, but represents the same idea to all nations and at all times. He is of opinion that one symbol does not represent two events, unless it first have a reference to some less event which is typical of some more important event; in that case, all together may be figurative of some great ultimate end. Although one symbol is supposed never to represent two different things, yet two or more symbols generally represent one thing. He has found by tracing back a symbol to its first use, that its true meaning is generally manifest. Since examining the Scriptures with this view he has been irresistibly drawn into the conclusions now exhibited.

The children of Israel were separated from all the nations of the earth and set apart to be holy unto the Lord. As they were in covenant with the God of Israel, he addressed them in the endearing character of a husband. Whenever they made any covenant or formed a confederacy with the nations around them, or imitated their idolatrous abominations, they were charged with spiritual whoredom. The church, under the gospel dispensation, is redeemed from amongst men out of every nation, and sanctified and set apart to be a peculiar people to show forth the praises of God. It is styled the Bride, the Lamb's wife. Its members are not to be conformed to this world but to be transformed by the renewing of the Spirit. They do not belong to any earthly kingdom, for our Lord has said, "They are not of the world, even as I am not of the world"; but they are citizens of the heavenly Zion and belong to the household of God; they are members of the same community, with the innumerable company of angels and the spirits of just men made perfect; and are to be governed by the very same spirit and temper which reigns amongst those blessed inhabitants above. God is an overflowing and unbounded ocean of blessedness and love; love is therefore the fulfilling of the law.

Whenever the subjects of the Redeemer unite themselves to the kingdoms of this world, and engage in their political contentions and fightings, then it appears they commit spiritual whoredom, for they forsake the fountain of living waters and hew out to themselves cisterns, — broken cisterns, which can hold no water.

When they thus mingle with the world and unite in its pursuits they may spiritually be styled adulterers.

The apostle James, while reproving the twelve tribes, which were scattered abroad, for their wars and fightings and friendship to the world, styles them adulterers and adulteresses. In direct opposition to this representation, the first fruits of the church are styled virgins, as not being defiled with women. "These are they which were not defiled with women; for they are virgins. These are they which follow the Lamb whithersoever he goeth. These were redeemed from amongst men, being the firstfruits unto God and the Lamb. And in their mouth was found no guile: for they are without fault before the throne of God." As virgins are pure and undefiled, so were the disciples of Christ in the first age of the church when they had no impure intercourse with the kingdoms of this world and followed the Lamb in refusing to engage either in its profits, honors, or fightings. They are, therefore, called virgins, without fault, in opposition to those who mingle with the world, who are spiritually styled harlots.

It evidently appears, if what has been said is true, that mystical Babylon, that mother of harlots and abominations of the earth, is just as extensive as the union of the church with the kingdoms of this world; and just in that proportion in which an individual Christian, or a single church, or a number of churches united in one body, engage in the honors, profits, and fightings of the kingdoms of this world, just in that proportion they may be said to be guilty of spiritual whoredom.

The writer is well aware that this inference, however just, will be looked upon with contempt by worldly political Christians whose dearest interest is involved in the kingdoms of this world, and especially by those who are clothed in purple and scarlet and have a golden cup in their hands. He has no expectation of being candidly heard by such, but it is God's own dear children who have ignorantly mingled with the world, having been blinded by their education, from whom he expects a candid hearing. "If any man have ears to hear, let him hear."

It is not common for a lewd woman openly to avow to the world her character; neither can it be expected that the mother of harlots will own her name. The writer is of opinion that very few have understood the full dimensions of this mystical city; she appears to him in her greatest extent to be bounded but little short of the whole visible church of God. She is styled "the *great City*, which spiritually is called Sodom and Egypt, where also our Lord was crucified." "And in her was found the blood of prophets and saints and of all that were slain upon the earth." But a dreadful judgment awaits her: "She shall utterly be burnt with fire: for strong is the Lord God who judges her." Being mingled with the nations and supported by their power, when they become like stubble before the devouring fire, she will be consumed with them. The whore is represented as riding upon a scarlet-colored beast, and upheld by him.[1]

[1] The writer is fully of opinion that a ferocious beast is never used as a symbol of a corrupt church, but of a tyrannical warlike power.

When he, with all his heads, are cast into the lake of fire, she will likewise be given to the burning flame. But before this great and dreadful day of the Lord shall come, which will burn as an oven, when the whore shall be consumed with the nations of the earth, God will call to his people to come out of her, saying unto them, "Come out of her, my people, that ye be not partakers of her sins, and that ye receive not of her plagues." As God's ancient people were carried captives into literal Babylon, so God's dear people will be found captives in mystical Babylon, until they hear the command of their Lord to come out of her that they be not partakers of her sins and that they receive not of her plagues. The captive daughters of Zion are very numerous. O that they may soon arise and shake themselves from the dust! "Shake thyself from the dust; arise, and sit down, O Jerusalem: loose thyself from the bands of thy neck, O captive daughter of Zion."

5. If the Mediator's kingdom is not of this world, and the kingdoms of this world are under the dominion of Satan, and if Christ's subjects cannot unite themselves to the kingdoms of this world, without committing spiritual whoredom, then we may infer the great impropriety of the subjects of the Mediator's kingdom

He has been for some time of opinion that the second Apocalyptic beast is rising, and that he will possess all the power of the first beast before him, and that under him the false prophet will appear; and the witnesses will be slain; and upon his kingdom the six first vials of his divine wrath will be principally poured out; and the seventh will be poured upon Satan's kingdom universally, as he is the prince of the power of the air.

becoming political Christians and enrolling themselves with the men of this world. They cannot serve two masters: for they will either hate the one, and love the other; or else they will hold to the one, and despise the other.

How humiliating is it to see subjects of the King of Zion engaged in the drudgery of the prince of darkness, laboring and struggling to support his tottering throne! Satan's kingdom is divided against itself and must, therefore, come to an end. But how lamentable is it to see the sons of the living God, the subjects of the Prince of Peace, taking sides in the cause of the adversary of souls, and actually opposing and fighting each other under his banner! They do it ignorantly and will, therefore, obtain forgiveness, for they know not what manner of spirit they are of. They are commanded to have no fellowship with the unfruitful works of darkness, but rather reprove them.

Before our Lord departed from this world to go to the Father, he gave laws to his subjects for their rule of life until his second coming. All these laws contemplated their residing as a holy nation in the midst of a wicked and benighted world, to reflect the rays of the Sun of righteousness on the thick darkness which covers the people. They were to be a city set upon a hill and a light to the world. The apostle exhorts them to "do all things without murmurings and disputings: that ye may be blameless and harmless, the sons of God, without rebuke, in the midst of a crooked and perverse nation, among whom ye shine as lights in the world." They must be a peculiar people to show forth the praises of God. How inconsistent is it, then, for the citizens of the heavenly Zion to be mingling with the politicians of this world and uniting in their processions, feasts, and cabals, when they ought rather to be praying for them, that the very sins they commit in these scenes may be forgiven them! Dear brethren, is it not high time to come out from the world and be separated? "Be ye not unequally yoked together with unbelievers: for what fellowship hath righteousness with unrighteousness? and what communion hath light with darkness? and what concord hath Christ with Belial?" "Wherefore come out from among them, and be ye separate, saith the Lord, and touch not the unclean thing; and I will receive you, and will be a Father to you, and ye shall be my sons and daughters, saith the Lord Almighty."

6. In view of what has been said, we finally infer that every interest which is not built upon the sure foundation stone which God has laid in Zion will be swept away when the storms of divine wrath shall beat upon our guilty world. "For, behold, the day cometh, that shall burn as an oven; and all the proud, yea, and all that do wickedly, shall be stubble: and the day that cometh shall burn them up, saith the Lord of hosts, that it shall leave them neither root nor branch." "For the day of the Lord of hosts shall be upon every one that is proud and lofty, and upon every one that is lifted up; and he shall be brought low." "The lofty looks of man shall be humbled, and the haughtiness of men shall be bowed down; and the Lord alone shall be exalted in

that day." "The Lord at thy right hand shall strike
through kings in the day of his wrath. He shall judge
among the heathen, he shall fill the places with their
dead bodies; he shall wound the head over many countries." "For, behold, the Lord will come with fire, and
with his chariots like a whirlwind, to render his anger
with fury, and his rebuke with flames of fire. For by
fire and by his sword will the Lord plead with all flesh:
and the slain of the Lord shall be many." "For
the indignation of the Lord is upon all nations, and
his fury upon all their armies: he hath utterly destroyed them, he hath delivered them to the slaughter.
Their slain shall be cast out, and their stink shall
come up out of their carcasses, and the mountains
shall be melted with blood." "For this is the day of
the Lord God of hosts, a day of vengeance, that he
may avenge him of his adversaries: and the sword
shall devour, and it shall be satiate and be made drunk
with their blood." The nations must drink of the
wine of the wrath of God, which shall be poured out
without mixture, into the cup of his indignation; and
they will be trodden in the great wine press of the
wrath of God Almighty. And the great whore which
has drunk the blood of the saints and the blood of
the martyrs of Jesus will have blood to drink; for
she is worthy.

The sword of the Lord has two edges; it will cut
off the offending limbs of the church and destroy
her enemies. The fire of the Lord will purify his
saints but utterly burn up the wicked. He "whose
fan is in his hand will thoroughly purge his floor, and

gather his wheat into the garner; but he will burn up the chaff with unquenchable fire." Although the earth is thus to be desolated, and the nations destroyed, yet the saints of the Most High shall "possess the kingdom for ever and ever." "And the kingdom and dominion, and the greatness of the kingdom under the whole heaven, shall be given to the people of the saints of the Most High, whose kingdom is an everlasting kingdom, and all dominions shall serve and obey him."

Dear brethren, these events are rapidly rolling in the fiery wheels down the descent of time; and although the nations must first drink the vials of divine wrath and the battle of God Almighty must first be fought, yet the time is at hand when we shall no more hear the sound of war, and of garments rolled in blood, for man will cease to be the enemy of man, and every one will sit quietly under his own vine and under his own fig tree; and there will be nothing to hurt or destroy in all God's holy mountain, and the knowledge of the Lord shall cover the earth as the waters cover the channels of the mighty deep.

Dear brethren, is it not "high time to awake out of sleep: for now is our salvation nearer than when we believed. The night is far spent, the day is at hand: let us therefore cast off the works of darkness, and let us put on the armour of light." And let us pray with all prayer and supplication in the Spirit for all men, not only for ourselves, our families, and our friends, and the church of God, but for a dying world, that God would in infinite compassion cut short these days of dreadful calamity for his elect's sake; and in the midst of deserved wrath remember mercy.

"He that hath ears to hear, let him hear what the Spirit saith unto the churches; To him that overcometh will I give to eat of the tree of life, which is in the midst of the paradise of God."

THE

LAWFULNESS OF WAR

FOR CHRISTIANS,

EXAMINED

⸻

BY JAMES MOTT.

⸻

" Ye are my friends, if ye do whatsoever I command you."

JOHN, XV. 14.

" If ye love me, keep my commandments."

JOHN, XIV. 15.

⸻

NEW-YORK :

PRINTED AND SOLD BY SAMUEL WOOD,

No. 357, Pearl-street.

⸻

1814.

Lawfulness of War

CHRISTIANS,

EXAMINED.

———

The object of the following remarks, is to endeavour to remove the prejudices of those who, through the influence of education, custom, or public opinion, have been induced to conclude that war is allowable for christians.

The writer acknowledges himself indebted for the principal part of what he has penned, to authors of different religious sentiments, in some points, but who all agree that war is opposed to christianity.— From these, he has taken some passages verbatim ; condensed others ; and occasionally interspersed his own ideas.

The consequences and miseries of war, are thus described by the learned Erasmus ; who wrote about 300 years ago.

" If there is in the affairs of mortal men, any one thing, which it is proper uniformly to explode ; which it is incumbent on every man, by every lawful means, to deprecate, to oppose ; that one thing is, doubtless, war. There is nothing more unnaturally wicked, more productive of misery, more extensively destructive, more obstinate in mischief, more unworthy of man, as formed by nature, much more of man professing christianity. Yet, wonderful to relate, in these times, war is every where rashly, and on the slightest pretext, undertaken ; cruelly and savagely conducted, not only by unbelievers, but by professed christians.

" Man has arrived at such a degree of insanity, that wars seem to be the great business of human life. Nations are almost always at war, either in preparation or action. Nation rises against nation, and, what even the heathens would have reprobated as unnatural, relatives against their nearest kindred, brother against brother, son against father ; more atrocious still, a christian against a man; and worst of all, a christian against a christian !

" To me, it appears to deserve a worse name than brutal : it is more than brutal, when men engage in the conflict of arms ; ministers of death to men ! Most of the brutes live in concord with their own kind. Lions, with all their fierceness, are quiet among themselves : Dragons are said to live in peace with Dragons : and even venomous creatures live with one another in perfect harmony. But to man, no wild beast is more destructive than his fellow man.

" When the brutes fight, they fight with weapons nature gave them ; we arm ourselves for mutual slaughter,with weapons which nature never thought of ; but which were invented by the contrivance of some accursed fiend, the enemy of human nature ; that man might become the destroyer of man. Man with man, and any man with any man, can find an everlasting cause for contest, and become what they call, natural enemies."

By war, fathers and sons, husbands and brothers, have rolled in blood by tens of thousands. For what ? Let us pause, and, blushing for man's depravity, inquire, for what this effusion of human blood ? For what, this slaughter and rapine that reduce thousands to wretchedness ? Such scenes must soften the heart that is not steeled against the cries of the distressed. But while the tear of sympathy for the living, steals involuntarily from the eye, the contemplation of the quick transition of the dead, is awful : and, when viewing them as rushing on with the rage of demons to meet the fatal stroke, that disunites the soul and body, more awful still to contemplate the state of these unbodied souls.

By war, laws are compelled to silence ; charity is laughed at ; youth is corrupted by every species of vice ; and contempt of piety and general corruption of principle and morals, are its attendants. And yet, wonderful to relate, there are many who argue with such a degree of plausibility, in favour of what they call defensive war, that even pious people are led into a persuasion that it is justifiable for christians to engage in it, *for the safety and defence of themselves, their country, liberties, civil rights, &c.* alleging, that self-defence is the first law of nature ; and that custom and the laws of nations, dictate to repel force by force : can christianity, therefore, say they, forbid it ? To which let it be replied,

1. That the author of the christian Religion fully answered the query, " can christianity forbid it ?" when he said, " Ye have heard that it hath been said, an eye for an eye, and a tooth for a tooth : but I say unto you, that ye resist not evil : but whosoever shall smite thee on thy right cheek, turn to him the other also." "If ye forgive not men their trespasses, neither will your heavenly Father forgive your trespasses." How clearly does Christ here point out the change from the Jewish law, to his own divine law of peace and forbearance ; and inculcates the principles of forgiveness and nonresistance, forbidding every kind of retaliation, or any thing like repelling force by force !

2. Custom and the laws of nations cannot be a certain criterion by which to judge of the truth of a position ; because, they are fallible. Custom is changeable, and often erroneous. Professed christian warriors now detest former customs, of putting all prisoners of war to the sword, or making slaves of them : and, had the laws of kingdoms or nations always been consistent with the nature of christianity, they would never have condemned the martyrs to the

1 *

flames, nor the Africans to cruel slavery. Thus, as laws of nations as well as custom, appear to have been erroneous, they afford no support to the advocates for war.

3. Self-defence, it is said, is the first law of nature; but it is of nature only : it belongs solely to the animal life ; and the brute creation knowing no further, act up to the perfection of their nature. Had man, like them, no higher privilege than mortal existence, he might be right in following their example : but man is a rational creature, and has an immortal soul to guard from every taint of guilt, and disobedience to his Maker's will: consequently, if duty to his God call for it, he is to give up all, even his natural life. "He that loses his life for my sake, shall find it," saith the Saviour.— Thus the martyrs yielded their backs to the scourge, their breasts to the sword of the executioner, and their bodies to the flames, without resistance or a murmur : even praying for their murderers. And some of these died for refusing to fight. But men are not only rational creatures : those who lay claim to christianity, profess to be governed by Christian principles. Yet, let it be remembered, that we are no further governed by christian principles, than as we are influenced by Christ's spirit, follow his example, and adhere to his precepts. Is there to be found any thing like self-defence, in any instance of his conduct? Or, do we read in any of his precepts, a command, or even liberty to destroy men's lives in our own or country's defence? Quite the reverse. He is emphatically called the Prince of Peace : and the whole of his example, and all his precepts lead to peace and nonresistance.

How decided Christ's language! "My kingdom is not of this world : if my kingdom were of this world, then would my servants fight, that I should not be delivered to the Jews." How natural the inference, that if we are his servants, influenced by his spirit, we cannot fight. But he not only urges christians to the negative virtue of forbearance, but to the positive duty of love. "Ye have heard that it hath been said, thou shalt love thy neighbour, and hate thine enemy ; but I say unto you, love your enemies, bless them that curse you, do good to them that hate you, and pray for them that despitefully use you, and persecute you." And why ? "That ye may be the children of your Father which is in heaven."

Give the preceding scripture passages their full scope, and can the principle of war be supported for a moment ? The voice of impartiality, of religion, of humanity, all unite to declare, how forced a meaning must be supplied, to make them breathe any thing but love, peace, good will and harmony to the sons of men. If christianity inspires with these pacific dispositions, the plea for war, to defend our liberties, civil rights, and even life itself, falls to the ground ; for war cannot be undertaken in this temper of mind : it cannot be carried on in the spirit of love.

4. Our liberties and civil rights, are certainly blessings, while they can be enjoyed with innocence, or obtained without being purchased by a crime : but their value is not so important, as to warrant us to violate the doctrine of Christ, in order to defend them. They are blessings to us, only as we make a right use of them. At best, they relate to this life alone, and like the fashion of the world to which they belong, are rapidly passing away. A few fleeting years will close our eyes to all terrestrial objects, and place us beyond the reach of worldly privilege or advantage ; and then, what will be their value to us ? Man can carry nothing with him when he dieth, but the register of an approving or guilty conscience : and can any professed christian, even in defence of his liberties, with this command imprinted on his mind, "love thine enemy, and render to him good for evil; "thrust his fellow creature through the heart, and hurry him to the awful tribunal of his judge, with an approving conscience ?

To be instrumental in sending men into eternity, is a very awful thing; but, it is to be feared, it claims too little of the serious attention of mankind ; either as it respects the consequences to themselves, or destiny of those who are slain by their hand.

Where are there so many and sacred obligations to love and perfect concord, as in the Christian religion? Where such numerous exhortations to peace ? And what practice among mankind, violates the law of love and peace so grossly as war ? Christ salutes his disciples with the happy omen of peace; he leaves them the legacy of peace. " Peace I leave with you ; my peace I give unto you: not as the world giveth, give I unto you." In his prayer, the subject of his devout entreaty was principally, that, as he was one with the Father, so his disciples, (that is, all christians) might be one with him. This union is something more than peace, more than friendship, more than concord ; it is an intimate communion with the divine nature. Kind Providence has given to man a spark of the divine mind, which stimulates him, without any hope of reward, and of his own free will, to do good to all ; for of God, this is the most natural, and appropriate attribute, to consult the good of all, by disinterested beneficence. If it were not so, how does it happen, that we feel an exquisite delight, when we find that any person has been preserved from danger, injury or destruction, by our offices or intervention ? Is it not matter of astonishment that man, thus formed for peace and good will ; formed to promote the welfare of all around him, should rush on, with mad ferocity, to the destruction of himself and his fellow creatures ?

At the nativity of Christ, the angels sung not the glories of war, nor a song of triumph, but a hymn of peace. Glory to God in the highest, on earth peace, good will toward men. The words and works of Christ are in perfect unison : as two undeniable witnesses, they join in bearing the most conclusive evidence against all fury, contention and strife. Examine every part of his doctrine, and nothing will be found that does not breathe peace, speak the language of love, and savour of charity. He was meek and lowly, and he enjoins us to be so too. In short, as the whole of his doctrine inculcates forbearance and love, so his life taught nothing but mildness, gentleness, and kind affection.

Two of the disciples, while yet under their Jewish prejudices, addressed our Saviour, " Lord wilt thou that we command fire to come down from Heaven and consume them, even as Elias did ?" May christians bear in mind his answer : " Ye know not what spirit ye are of, for the Son of man came not to destroy men's lives, but to save them." Christians censure unbelievers: but can any thing tend more to confirm them in their unbelief, than the mutual slaughter of men professing to be governed by the christian spirit ; the spirit of love, peace and forbearance ?

That the precepts and doctrine of Christ apply to and are binding on christians in their individual capacity, will, it is presumed, be acceded to by all: consequently, if individuals are bound to act up to certain principles, because they are christians ; nations composed of these individuals, are subject to the same rules ; and, if they transgress the commands of Christ, are answerable therefor, equally with an individual. The two common distinction between political expediency, and christian duty, is a distinction dangerous in the extreme ; not founded in truth, and of most pernicious tendency to morality in general. Therefore, it behoves men to examine carefully, the dangerous consequence of lessening the moral obligation of Scripture precepts ; or making the commands of Christ equivocal. For truly, if the command to love enemies, to do good for evil, and not resist evil; does not extend to political bodies of Christians, all consistency is at an end. Individual responsibility for conduct will be taken from man. Crimes clearly marked and defined in the Bible, will cease to be crimes at the will of princes or rulers ; and men will have two different standards of morality ; one, the command of the gospel, the other, the orders of governments or customs of the world. But, be it remembered, that neither orders of government, nor customs of the world will take away individual responsibility.

But some say, if these pacific principles prevail, our liberties and civil rights will be torn from us; and we shall become a prey to every invader. Surely not, unless the Lord hath forsaken the earth, and forgotten his people; for the Psalmist declares, " whoso putteth his trust in the Lord shall be safe." But, from whence ariseth the dread of being destroyed by our enemies, if we do not go to war with them? Does it not indicate a disbelief in the superintendance of divine Providence? And that we place greater confidence in man for protection, than in the Supreme Almighty Governor, in whose hands are the issues of life and death? Whence cometh distrust of his providential care over us, but from a consciousness of disobedience, and consequent guilt? For God's promises are all yea and amen forever; and he has promised, " If ye walk in my statutes, and keep my commandments, I will give you peace in your land, and ye shall lie down, and none shall make you afraid." The Saviour's language is equally encouraging, " not a sparrow is forgotten before God, but even the very hairs of your heads are all numbered; fear not, therefore; ye are of more value than many sparrows." The apostle Peter's doctrine is similar, " The eyes of the Lord are over the righteous, and his ears are open to their prayers. And who is he that will harm you, if ye be followers of that which is good? But, and if ye suffer for righteousness sake, happy are you : be not afraid of their terror, neither be troubled, but sanctify the Lord God in your hearts." Will not a firm belief in these express promises, do away all distrust of Providential protection? Were the minds of mankind brought into a true christian state, the protection of divine Providence would humbly and safely be relied upon : but while they suffer avarice, ambition, and revenge, to influence them, they will always find a pretext for war: and in these dispositions, they cannot trust divine Providence; and, indeed, they have no right to expect his protection.

A remarkable instance of the protecting care of the great Preserver of men, we are furnished with, in the injunction and promise to the Jews: " Thrice in the year shall your males appear before the Lord." (at Jerusalem) " Neither shall any man desire your land, when ye shall go up to appear before the Lord your God thrice in the year." Which promise, Josephus the Jewish historian informs, was so punctually fulfilled, that though their enemies knew these stated times, and that their cities were defenceless, yet at these seasons, they were never invaded: " The terror of the Lord being upon the cities round about them."

A recent account of the effects of reliance on Providential protection, instead of the arm of flesh, we have in the settlement of Pennsylvania. Its first European inhabitants, were principled against fighting. They accordingly did not provide themselves with any weapons of defence, though surrounded by nations of warlike Indians; among whom they lived in harmony, during the time they had the reins of government in their hands, which was about 70 years— while the other provinces were involved in almost continual warfare with the natives.*

The reply of John the Baptist to the soldiers, " do violence to no man, and be content with your wages," is sometimes advanced in support of war: but let all soldiers take this advice; " do violence to no

* William Penn, although made proprietor of Pennsylvania by a grant from king Charles the 2d, did not consider this a sufficient title, while the land was in possession of its native inhabitants.— He therefore, consistently with the christian's law, of " doing unto all men, as we would they should do unto us," purchased of them their right: and as he wished to extend his settlements, he continued to make purchases, and thus obtained their confidence, and maintained peace.

man," and there will be an end of wars. And should it be granted (which we have no grounds for) that John tolerated war; yet this is not to the point, as he was under the dispensation of the law, when to love enemies had not been taught mankind.

Another argument advanced, is the expression of our Saviour to his disciples, "He that hath no sword, let him sell his garment and buy one." That the disciples understood this direction literally, as they had done some of his other sayings, which were not meant so, is evident by the reply they made ; " here are two swords;" of which it does not appear that he took any further notice than to say " it is enough." Were only two sufficient for their defence ? But does not our Lord's reproving Peter for cutting off the ear of Malchus ; by healing the wound, and ordering the sword to be put into its sheath, with the addition of this denunciation, " all they that take the sword, shall perish with the sword," render this passage a decided testimony against war, even in self-defence ? That Christ intended by this direction, that the " ambassadors of peace," his apostles, should arm themselves with weapons of destruction to man, I can form no idea of.

Can it be supposed, that the blessed Messiah, after so positively forbidding the indulgence of every disposition that would lead into strife and contention, should command his followers to provide weapons to defend themselves with, which they could not use for that purpose, without the aid of those very passions which he had prohibited ? The New Testament does not furnish an instance, (except the reprehended one of Peter's) of an apostle or disciple using a sword or weapon of defence. The doctrine of the apostles is in perfect unison with that of their divine Master. Paul charges the Romans, " recompense to no man evil for evil. Be patient in tribulation : bless them that persecute you : bless and curse not : overcome evil with good." Similar is the language of Peter, who, after charging to lay aside all malice, guile and envy; adds, " If when ye do well, and suffer for it, ye take it patiently, this is acceptable with God. For even hereunto were ye called; because Christ also suffered for us, leaving us an example, that ye should follow his steps ; who, when he was reviled, reviled not again ; when he suffered, he threatened not ; but committed himself to him that judgeth righteously." 1 Pet. ii. 1, 20, 21, 23. John's language is, " We should love one another; not as Cain, who was of that wicked one, and slew his brother." " God is love, and he that dwelleth in love, dwelleth in God, and God in him. There is no fear in love ; but perfect love casteth out fear. If a man say, I love God, and hateth his brother, he is a liar." 1 John, iii. 11, 12, iv. 16, 18, 20. Indeed the New Testament throughout, breathes the language of love, peace, long-suffering and charity.

And we are informed by authentic history,* that the christians of the first two centuries, were so clothed with the spirit of love, and by it introduced into such a tender feeling for mankind, that they unanimously refused to fight, or go to war on any occasion ; although for refusing, grievous sufferings were the consequence ; and even loss of life itself to some. If we compare their conduct with that of christians of the present day, who, though making the same profession of religion, yet advocate war ; is there any alternative, but to conclude, that those early followers were in an error, or that they who advocate war now, are in one ; or that time has changed the nature of the gospel ?

Professing christians in the more corrupt ages since, having engaged in war, can by no means justify those of the present day ; because, if example is to be followed, it ought to be the example of those, who lived nearest the commencement of the christian era, and whose conduct in refusing to fight, is certainly

* See Appendix.

most consistent with the doctrines of the New Testament.

It is indeed lamentable, that men, and even men of penetrating minds, should suffer themselves to be so influenced by prevailing custom and public opinion, as to conclude that war is allowable ; without investigating whether these are consonant with the principles of christianity.

But says the justifier of war, "If wars had been absolutely unlawful, God would not have commanded the Jews to wage war against their enemies." To this plea it may be replied, first, That various have been the dispensations of Providence to men. Many things were by the Mosaic law, enjoined on the Jews, that were not on the Gentile nations. Many are enjoined on Christians that were not on Jews by their law. The legal dispensation did not command to love enemies, and do good for evil. Thus, it is evident, that the object of the gospel dispensation, was a greater perfection of the human character, than the law of Moses contemplated : therefore, for christians to whom new commandments of a higher nature are given ; to descend to a practice of the Jews, in opposition to their new command, is as unjustifiable, as it would have been for Jews to have adopted heathen customs forbidden by their law.

Secondly. The Jews went to war at the command of God, and against nations, whom for their wickedness, he, in his inscrutable wisdom, had determined to extirpate from the earth. But it was only at his immediate command that they were to do it. Have professing christians received similar commands, to destroy nations ? Or rather, do they not fight at the command of their passions ? And is it not by a thirst for riches and glory, some disputed claim, or causes more trifling, that the flames of war are often kindled, and thousands of lives sacrificed ? But why do christians pitch upon the Jews' warlike actions, as the only model for imitation ? Why not practice circumcision ? Why not sacrifice cattle ? Admit plurality of

wives? If we disapprove these practices, as not com-
porting with the dispensation of the gospel; let us,
for the same reasons, disapprove following their example relative to war; that destroyer of life, religion
and morals, and entailer of misery and distress on
millions that are left to deplore its consequences.

It is worthy of notice, that David, endeared as he
was by his virtues; yet, because " he had shed
much blood, and made great wars," was forbidden to
build the temple.* Although the wars that he carried on, were at the command of the Lord, and
against the wicked; and though neither he nor the
rest of mankind, had been taught, that they ought to
love enemies; the building of a house to the Lord, was
reserved for Solomon, whose name signifies pacific.

For Christians to plead Jewish example to justify
them in wars, is but a fig-leaf covering: for, if they
properly reflect, they must see, that the Jews prac-
tising war, even among themselves, is no plea for it,
under the gospel; because, as hath been observed, the
Mosaic law did not command to love enemies, forgive
injuries, and do good for evil. These are commands that appertain to the higher, to the gospel dispensation, when swords are to be beaten into ploughshares. Christ's divine law, is so far from allowing
to kill, that it forbids to cherish the passion of revenge. Thus, in his allusion to the Mosaic law, he
says," Ye have heard that it hath been said, an eye for
an eye, and a tooth for a tooth; but I say unto you, that
ye resist not evil, but whosoever shall smite thee on
thy right cheek, turn to him the other also. Ye have
heard that it hath been said, thou shalt love thy
neighbour and hate thine enemy; but I say unto
you, love your enemies, bless them that curse you,
and do good to them that hate you, and pray for
them that despitefully use you, and persecute you.
For if ye love them which love you, what reward

* 1, Chron. xxii. 8.

have you? and if ye salute your brethren only, what
do you more than others? Be ye therefore perfect,
even as your father which is in heaven is perfect."
What a clear distinction between the law and the gospel is here pointed out! How much greater purity is
required of Christians than was of Jews, to whom the
commands of love and forbearance were never given!
And as our Lord's commandments and promises remain to be inseparable, nothing but a compliance with
his injunctions, can give a claim to his promises.

Since the time that Jesus Christ said, " put up
thy sword into its sheath," christians ought not to go
to war : unless it be in that most honourable warfare,
with the vilest enemies of the church, and of man's
happiness, revenge, lust, ambition, pride and the in-
ordinate love of money.   These are our Canaanites,
Amorites, Hittites and Jebusites ; with whom we
ought never to make a truce. With these we must engage without intermission ; till, the enemy being utterly extirpated, peace may be finally established.   Unless we subdue such enemies as these, we can neither
have peace with ourselves, nor peace with others.
He who shall have conquered foes like these, will
never wish to wage war with any mortal upon that
earth, on which God placed man to live, and let live,
and enjoy the life he gave.

Notwithstanding the peculiar excellency of the
gospel is, that it brings peace and good will to men ; not
merely to friends and neighbours, but to men—mankind ; yet, astonishing to relate, men professing to be
influenced and governed by it, have been led along,
as it were blindfold, by custom and example, in the
inhuman practice of killing and destroying each
other, without thinking it a crime.

How very instructive, that the descent of the divine spirit upon our Saviour, was in the likeness of
the innocent, inoffensive dove! what emblem more
significant of its nature and tendency! and how fully
his meek, unresisting conduct proves its effect! does
it influence men differently, that they, though pro-

fessing to be his followers, governed by this dove-like spirit, can be cruel, wrathful destroyers of each other?

How irreconcilable, that in one age christians are recorded to have been meek and lowly followers of their suffering Lord; and, like him, submitting to every indignity rather than contend; in another age, men under the same religious profession, claiming the same crucified Christ for their leader; appear in all the horrid pomp of military parade, and contend even at the expense of the lives of thousands and tens of thousands!

But, notwithstanding men act as they do, in killing each other, real christianity has ever been, and ever will be the same; and must necessarily produce the same fruits; which an inspired apostle tells us, are "love, joy, peace, long-suffering, gentleness, goodness, faith, meekness." Can any man possessing these, buckle on the harness to kill or to be killed? Let us not deceive ourselves, nor be deceived; God is not mocked; but whatever a man soweth, that shall he also reap.

Such indeed are the dreadful consequences of war, that it is no marvel that the apostle James had to declare their origin. "From whence come wars and fightings? Come they not hence, even of your lusts?" And of all lusts, can there be any more detestable, than that which produces the selfish, revengeful disposition to injure others?

I cannot conceive how the crime of murder, which is considered of the highest magnitude in an individual, can lose its criminality when authorised by the rulers of any people. If a man, to revenge an insult, kill another, the horrid deed is resounded through the country, and he suffers death for the crime: but if a chief ruler, under the same pretext, viz. insult, for months matures his plans for slaughter, and by his order thousands are murdered, praises for his (so called) glorious deeds, are vociferated from shore to shore. There is, however, this difference; though

2 *

both act from the same principle, and are alike influenced by malice, one is legalized by government, the other is condemned by the same. But let it not be forgotten, that malice and revenge are forbidden by high authority, whether indulged by prince or peasant. 1 Pet. ii. 1, and Rom. xii. 19.

As it is the nature of all evil, that its malignity increases the more it is extended; therefore, if it is inhuman, if it is wicked, for one man to meet another with a sword pointed at his vitals ; how much is the mass of inhumanity and wickedness increased, when thousands and tens of thousands meet in the same manner, and either slay without mercy, or fall without pity !

A man is justly accounted infamous who steals a coat ; but if the same man engages in war, and after shedding blood, returns from the battle laden with the property of many innocent men, he is ranked amongst honest and reputable members of society. I cannot conceive how the infamous practice of robbing, can lose its infamy, by adding murder to it, though authorised by government ; unless government has power to remove the criminality of that which God has made a crime. What but wicked custom, justifies government more than individuals, in robbing and plundering ?

The love of our country,* is a plea frequently urged in favour of defensive war. But what is the love of our country, if opposed to the law of Christ, but a blind and selfish attachment to that particle of earth on which we happen to live ? The benevolence of a christian mind is not confined within such nar-

* " Christianity in its regards, steps beyond the narrow bounds of national advantage, in quest of universal good ; it does not encourage particular patriotism in opposition to general benignity ; or prompt to love our country at the expense of our integrity ; or allow us to indulge our passions to the detriment of thousands. It looks upon all the human race as children of the same father, and wishes them equal blessings : in ordering us to do good, to love as brethren, to forgive injuries and to study peace ; it quite annihilates the disposition for martial glory, and utterly debases the pomp of war." Sermon on Isaiah ii. by Bishop Watson.

low limits ; he views all the inhabitants of the earth, in the light of immortal and accountable beings ; he considers them as his brethren ; and his language is, "far better for me to resign whatever I possess, than that one human being should be destroyed in its defence. All worldly enjoyments are trifles in my estimation, when compared with the life of one fellow creature. Sooner, therefore, than take the life of a fellow heir to immortality, and precipitate his soul into an awful eternity, let me be obliged to the charity of my country for support."

Can any man, whether of public or private character, who practically loves, and does good to an enemy at home, do otherwise than love his enemy in every other place ? The doctrines of the New Testament fix no geographical boundaries to love between man and man. All men being of the same Parent, are consequently brethren : who can love a brother and kill him ?

Doubtless, if man, in the most tried situation, surrounded by enemies, follow the example of the persecuted Emmanuel, " O ! my Father, if this cup may not pass away except I drink it, thy will be done," though he should fall a victim to the wrath of man, yet would he triumph in death : having the gracious promise, " he that loses his life for my sake, shall find it." Such a man, though not lacking courage, may by some be regarded as weak and cowardly, for not daring to lift up his hand against the life of his fellow creature : but what then ? Will the censure of a few frail, mistaken mortals divest his innocent spirit of the peaceful reflection, that he died without the guilt of shedding human blood ?

But what will be the reflections of the man, who in the very act of slaughtering others, when wrath and revenge fill his heart, is himself in a moment hurried into eternity, to receive his final sentence from that judge who has commanded him to love his enemies, and not resist evil ! Can his reflections for doing the very reverse, be consoling ? Or can a rational being suppose, that with these dispositions he can be happy in heaven, where all is peace and concord? If not, when, where, or how is he to be divested of them? Christ has declared, " if ye die in your sins, where I go ye cannot come." It is presumed, none will say wrath and revenge are not sinful. My brethren, these are momentous considerations! May they stimulate us to seek an inheritance in the kingdom of heaven, in preference to a vain and imaginary immortality in the applause of men.

One great means of keeping alive the spirit of war, is that partiality which we contract in our early education for the manners of pagan antiquity : from whence, we learn to adopt ideas of virtue, directly opposite to those which christianity teaches ; to be guided by laws of honour, which that abhors; to imitate characters, which that detests ; and to behold heroes, patriots, conquerors, and suicides with admiration, whose conduct that utterly condemns.— Christians reprobate pagan immorality and idolatry, and yet adopt their erroneous ideas of virtue. Thus the conduct of Brutus in the murder of Cæsar, and the action of Cato in the destruction of his own life, are extolled as virtuous and heroic deeds. Pagan ideas of morality and virtue, are no rule for Christians ; because, founded on their ignorance of Christian requisitions. Applause for warlike achievements, was congenial with the religion of pagans, many of whose Gods were made out of deceased heroes, supposed to be exalted to heaven, as a reward for the mischiefs which they had perpetrated upon earth. Not such the religion of the christian! his, seeks not applause, and is so far from encouraging to revenge injuries, that it commands to forgive them, as the condition of obtaining forgiveness himself.

It has been observed by some, that it is difficult to draw the line between defensive war, and that coercion used by the civil magistrates, in taking life on some occasions. How the civil magistrates obtained this power, is a question worth investigating. The people, from whom they derive all the power they possess, have no right to take their own lives, and consequently cannot transfer it to them. A man may transfer to others a right to control his person—to regulate his conduct—and exact his services; and for these, he may receive an equivalent : but what equivalent can he receive for his life ? Man's life is, therefore, his own to preserve, but not to transfer, or destroy. His life, his conscience, and day of probation are unalienable. I wish my fellow-citizens to examine carefully the propriety of taking life in any case.

As mankind are to become christians individually, and bear their testimony against evil of every kind ; they are not to remain in the practice of any thing they are convinced is wrong, because other men continue in it : therefore, a man who acts in warlike measures, contrary to his judgment, will no more be justified in the sight of his Maker for so doing, than for theft or drunkenness.

Let those, therefore, who have tender scruples against taking the lives of their fellow men, cherish those scruples, lest their feelings become hardened, and the avenues to the heart closed against the tender calls of love, and they be left so to act, as finally to have the sad reflection, that contrary to their understanding, they have slain a fellow creature. May these conscientious ones remember, that if war is an evil, every step towards it, is also an evil : and it is a salutary scripture command, " abstain from all appearance of evil." 1 Thes. v. 22.

The principle of nonresistance, leads to obedience to magistracy, in all cases where a man can justify his conscience in the sight of God : further than this, no power on earth can be just in exacting it ; nor any true follower of the Saviour, justified in yielding it. When governments interfere with the religious rights of subjects, and bind their consciences ; then christians are to endure any sufferings rather than by complying with the laws of men, violate their higher and supreme obligations to the eternal God. Thus by an invincible adherence to the doctrines and example of Christ, will be manifested, the power and excellency of those principles which induced them patiently and meekly to submit to the greatest sufferings, rather than commit the least evil.

I am aware that the apostle Paul's recommendation of subjection to rulers, to principalities and powers, is by some brought to prove that when rulers command to war, subjects must obey. But Paul says, rulers are not a terror to good works, but to evil doers. I trust these advocates for implicit obedience, will readily allow, that obedience to the dictates of conscience, is not an evil ; and, therefore, upon Paul's principles, not punishable. Magistrates commanding what conscience forbids, is the only ground upon which christians ought to refuse an active compliance : and while I wish all due subjection shewn to rulers, I also wish, that christians may meekly, yet manfully, support the dignity of the christian character, in obeying God rather than man ; and if sufferings are the consequence, patiently endure them.

To admit the idea of implicit obedience to magistracy, without regard to conscience, is to condemn the prophet Daniel, and those three Israelites who were cast into the lion's den for not obeying the king's decree ; as well as the holy martyrs, for not relinquishing their faith at the command of princes. But Paul's record of his own sufferings and imprisonment for conscience sake, sets aside the plea for implicit obedience. He also defines the christian's weapons of warfare in his time, and of course in every succeeding time, to be " not carnal, but mighty through God, to the bringing into captivity every thought to the obedience of Christ." Carnal and spiritual weapons will no more unite under the gospel dispensation, than iron and clay.

But who can avoid being shocked, at beholding some of those who undertake to instruct others in the doctrines of the gospel, accompanying an army, and stimulating those who rely on them for saving instruction, to deeds, at the bare mention of which, the heart of humanity recoils; and which fill their unhappy country with widows and orphans ! Who can think of these things without dreading the awful effects of such an apostacy from a religion, that never did, nor ever will breath any thing different from peace on earth, and good will toward men.

Now, let us figure to ourselves two armies of professing christians engaged in battle; and one of these professedly pious instructers in each, and both at the same time praying for the success of their respective armies; and, (as is natural to suppose,) that every bullet may do execution, if conquest cannot be obtained without: would not such prayers be an abomination in the sight of the divine Majesty ?

Among the serious evils of war, is one which seems to be little thought of, or regarded : that is, the thousands of young men, born into this world, that they may be born again of God, and become his sons, and fellow heirs with Christ ; who are robbed of the precious gift of life before age and experience have ripened their judgments for usefulness : and, peradventure, before they have known that obedience to the influence of God's spirit in their hearts, which is an indispensable qualification to die the death of the righteous; but have been forced or tempted, in the ardour of youth, and strength of sinful passions, to rush on to kill or be killed, with furious haste, apparently forgetting God, eternity and their own souls.

I will now call the attention of the reader, to what that great man Erasmus says respecting christians going to war with christians. "How could it ever enter our hearts, that a christian should imbrue his hands in the blood of a christian ? If a brother murders his brother, the crime is called fratricide : but a christian is more closely allied to a christian as such, than a brother by consanguinity ; unless the bonds of nature are stronger than the bonds of Christ ; which christians consistently with their faith, cannot allow :

how absurd then is it, that they should be constantly
at war with each other, who form but one family, the
church of Christ: who are members of the same body ; who boast of the same head, even Jesus Christ ;
who have one Father in Heaven, common to them all,
who grow in grace by the same spirit; who are initia-
ted into the same mysteries, and redeemed by the
same Saviour !

" Whence then the tumults of war among the children of peace ? Is it a mere fable, when Christ calls
himself the vine, and his disciples the branches ?
Who can conceive a branch divided against a branch
of the same tree ? Or is it an unmeaning assertion,
which the apostle Paul repeatedly made, that the
church is one body, united in its many members, and
adhering to one head, Christ Jesus ? Who ever beheld the eye contending with the hand?

" In the animal body, there is peace among all the
members. If any evil happen to one member, the
whole body affords its assistance. Can then the
mere animal connexion of nature in an animal body,
formed soon to perish, effect more in preserving harmony, than the union of the spirit in a mystical and
immortal body ? Is it without meaning that we pray,
according to the command of Christ, thy will be done,
on earth as it is in Heaven? In the kingdom of Heaven, there is perfect concord. But Christ intended,
that his church should be nothing less than a celestial
community, a heaven upon earth, men belonging to it
living as much as possible, according to the heavenly
kingdom, and hastening thither."

If the christian religion be a fable, why do not men
explode it ? Why do they glory in its name? But if
Christ be the way, the truth, and the life, and teaches them nonresistance, Luke, vi. 29, why do they
fight ? If they acknowledge Christ to be their Lord
and Master, who is love itself, and who taught nothing
contrary to love and peace ; let them exhibit his
model ; not by assuming his name, but by their lives
and conversations. Let them adopt the love of

peace, that Christ may recognize his own, as they recognize him to be the teacher of peace.

Before I close these remarks, I can but recur to the prophets, and notice the connected chain of love and peace that is held up to our view, from them down to the apostles, as the object of christianity. With what rapturous language do the prophets express themselves, when in prophetic vision, they speak of the gospel day, and coming of the Messiah! "Unto us a child is born, unto us a son is given; and the government shall be upon his shoulders, and his name shall be called Wonderful, Counsellor, the mighty God, the everlasting Father, the Prince of peace. Of the increase of his government and peace, there shall be no end. And he shall judge among the nations, and shall rebuke many people, and they shall beat their swords into ploughshares, and their spears into pruning hooks: nation shall not lift up sword against nation, neither shall they learn war any more." "The work of righteousness shall be peace, and the effect of righteousness, quietness and assurance for ever." How correspondent is the acclamation of the heavenly host at the birth of Christ! "Glory to God in the highest, on earth peace, good will toward men." The gospel in Scripture is styled "the gospel of peace:" the apostles, "ambassadors of peace:" and they teach, that "the fruits of the spirit, are peace and love." Christ's life was spent in doing good to all classes of mankind; the doctrine he taught was love, peace, and forgiveness of injuries; and he died praying for his persecutors: thus sanctioning his doctrine by example. Can any man after taking into view all these corroborating evidences of the object of christianity, entertain an idea that himself or others, distinguished by such dispositions, can be the slaves of passions, which lead to imbrue their hands in human blood? Only let conscience do its office, and there will be no difficulty in deciding.

3

May the warrior pause, reflect, and seriously consider, whether a declaration of war, made by the greatest human authority, is a sufficient warrant for him, on christian principles, to deprive his fellow man of life or property : and, whether it is possible to do either, in a disposition that harmonizes with the spirit of the gospel, and the precepts and example of a meek, self-denying Saviour. The inquiry is very interesting for every professing christian who approves of war, to make ; seeing the consequences, both as it respects the destruction of the lives and property of his fellow men, and his own eternal well-being, are very momentous. For indeed it is an awful reflection, that after a few fleeting years, perhaps days, we shall appear before him, who can neither be awed nor bribed ; to receive the irrevocable sentence of, " come ye blessed," or " go ye cursed." It will be unavailing then to plead the command of rulers, custom or example ; the turning point will be, whether we have, according to the best of our understanding, done the will of God as revealed unto us. Let that man who is sheltering himself under a declaration of war, or legal authority, in forcibly dispossessing men of their property ; or depriving them of that life God has given them ; and sending them uncalled, and probably unprepared, into an awful eternity ; solemnly query, am I, in so doing, fulfilling Christ's injunctions, of doing good to those who hate me, loving enemies, and forgiving injuries ?" Surely, his heart must condemn him, and the answer be, " I am not." Then, may he awfully bear in mind the emphatic declaration, " if thine heart condemn thee, God is greater and knoweth all things." " And will," the Saviour has declared, " reward every man according to his works."

May those who profess to be ministers of the gospel, and are by many considered the oracles of truth, solemnly query previous to giving the least countenance to war, " have I, unbiassed by education, custom or commonly received opinion, carefully examined, whether war and christianity can harmonize ? or, in other words, whether it is possible, that the meek and gentle spirit of the gospel, can so assimilate with the destructive spirit of war, as that a man can be actuated by both at the same time ?" It is a subject demanding special inquiry of this class of citizens, both as it regards themselves and the community ; lest they mislead the people, and it be said of them, as of some formerly ; "the leaders of the people cause them to err, and they that are led of them are destroyed."

APPENDIX.

———

Having stated in page 13, that the Christians of the first two centuries refused taking any part in the war, on account of its inconsistency with the spirit of christianity ; to confirm that statement, I subjoin the following extracts from the writings of the primitive christians, as quoted by Thomas Clarkson.

Justin the Martyr, one of the earliest writers of the second century, says, " the devil is the author of all war." A severe sentence, and made even at a time when wars were considered the most honourable profession, and leading to glory.

Tatian, and Clemens of Alexandria, men of high standing, speak decidedly against the lawfulness of war.

Tertullian strongly condemned the practice of bearing arms, as it related to Christians, saying, in his " dissertation on the worship of idols," "though the soldiers came to John, and received a certain form to to be observed ; and the centurion believed, yet Christ by disarming Peter, disarmed every soldier afterwards : for custom never sanctions an illicit act." And in his " soldier's garland," he says, " can a soldier's life be lawful, when Christ has pronounced, that he who lives by the sword shall perish by the sword ? And shall he, who is not to avenge his own wrongs, be instrumental in bringing others into chains, imprisonment, torments, death ?"

Cyprian, in his epistle to Donatus, after observing on the dismal prospect of seas beset with pirates, highways with robbers, encampments, marches, and all the terrible forms of war and bloodshed, says,

" when a single murder is committed, it shall be deemed a crime ; but that crime shall commence a virtue when committed under the shelter of public authority ; so that punishment is not rated by the measure of guilt, but the more enormous the size of the wickedness, so much greater the chance for impunity."

Lactantius, who lived some time after Cyprian, in his treatise concerning the true worship of God ; says, " it can never be lawful for a righteous man to go to war, whose warfare is in righteousness itself." And again, " it can never be lawful to kill a man, whose person the Divine Being designed to be sacred, as to violence."

Origen, Archelaus, Ambrose, Chrysostom, Jerom, Syril, and indeed, every christian writer of the second century, who notices the subject of war, makes it unlawful for christians.

These were the sentiments of the early christians ; what was their practice? Tertullian, in his discourse to Scapula, tells us, that in the wars between the Emperor Verus, and Avidius Crassus, and those of the Emperor Severus, with Clodius Albinus, between the years, 169 and 198, no christians were to be found in these armies, though they were largely extended, and christianity had reached all the places in which these armies were.

Clemens of Alexandria, gives the christians of his day, the appellation of " peaceable, or the followers of peace." Thus distinguishing them from the soldiers of his age : and says expressly, that those who were the followers of peace, used none of the instruments of war."

Athanagorus and other early writers, remark, that the christians in their time, abstained when they were struck, from striking again, and even refused to go to law with those who injured them. They also kept away from the shows of the gladiators, giving it as a reason, " lest we should become partakers of the murders committed there."

3 *

A case of refusal to fight, as recorded by Ruinart, is to the point. Maximilian, a young man, being brought before the tribunal in order to be enrolled as a soldier, Dion the proconsul, asked him his name: Maximilian replied, " why wouldst thou know my name, I am a christian, and cannot fight." On his refusal to comply, still asserting he was a christian, Dion replied, " bear arms or thou shalt die:" to which the youth replied, " I cannot fight if I die, I am not a soldier of this world, but a soldier of God." Dion said, " who has persuaded thee to behave thus?" Maximilian answered, " my own mind, and he who called me." Dion commanded, " take thy arms, and receive the mark." " I can receive no such mark," says Maximilian, " I have already the mark of Christ." Upon which, Dion replied, " I will send thee quickly to thy Christ." " Thou mayest do so," answered Maximilian, " but the glory will be mine." Dion then bade the officer mark him : but Maximilian still persisted in refusing, and spoke thus : " I am a christian, and it is not lawful to wear such a mark, when I have received the mark of the Lord Jesus Christ, the son of the living God, who died to give us life. Him all we christians obey : him we follow as the restorer of our life, and the author of our salvation." Dion said, " consider thy youth and bear arms : the profession of arms becomes a young man." He replied, " my arms are with the Lord ; I cannot fight for any earthly consideration : I am now a christian."

After further expostulating with him, but in vain, Dion ordered his name to be struck off the roll ; and then delivered the following sentence ; " Maximilian, because thou hast, with a rebellious spirit, refused to bear arms, thou art to die by the sword." This conscientious young man replied, " thanks be to God." Thus nobly did a youth of 20 years of age, bear testimony against war.

And as the early christians would not enter into the armies, so when the christian faith was embraced by some while in them, they relinquished the profession of arms. Marcellus was a centurion in the legion called Trajana. On a festival, he threw down his military belt, at the head of the legion, declaring that he would no longer serve in the army ; for that he had become a christian. " I hold in detestation," said he, " the worship of your Gods : Gods that are made of wood and stone ; Gods which are deaf and dumb :" and adds, "it is not lawful for a christian who is the servant of Christ the Lord, to bear arms for any earthly consideration." He was confined more than three months in prison, and then executed.

Tertullian, in his " soldier's garland," says, that many in his time " immediately on their conversion, quitted the military service." We are also told by Archelaus, who flourished under Probus, that many Roman soldiers, after having witnessed the piety and generosity of Marcellus, and having embraced christianity, immediately forsook the profession of arms. We are also told by Eusebius, that, about the same time, " numbers laid aside a military life, and became private persons, rather than abjure their religion." And Martin, of whom Sulpicius says so much, had been bred to the profession of arms, but on his conversion to christianity, declined it, saying, " I am a christian, and therefore I cannot fight."

Celsus, who lived at the end of the second century, attacked the christian religion ; charging its followers, among other things, with refusing to bear arms for the Emperor, even in cases of necessity ; saying, that if the rest of the empire were of their opinion, it would soon be overrun by the barbarians. Origen, who lived in the third century, admits in his answer to Celsus, that the christians would not bear arms, and justifies them for refusing, on the principle of the unlawfulness of war.

These early writers considered the prophecy that swords should be turned into ploughshares, &c. was in the act of completion in individuals of those times.

Irenæus, about the year 180, says, " the christians have changed their swords and their lances into instruments of peace, and they know not how to fight."

Justin Martyr, contemporary with Irenæus, asserts, that " the prophecy is fulfilled, you have good reason to believe, for we, who in times past killed one another, do not now fight with our enemies."

That there were no christian soldiers in the first and second century, is evident, and that christianity was then in its purest state, will, I trust, be granted by all.

Let us now trace their character, as given by Athanagorus, Justin Martyr, Minucius Felix, and others; and see how it squares with their principles and practice. " They were, say these writers, plain and frugal in their apparel and furniture, temperate in their eating and drinking; relinquished all the diversions of the times, which they saw had any tendency to evil; punctual to their words and engagements; lovers of truth, and of one another; kind, courteous and charitable to others, beyond example; abstained from all manner of violence, prayed for their enemies who persecuted them; were patterns of humility and patience; made no sacrifices of conscience, even to save their lives."

But in the third century, the christian discipline began to relax; and a degeneracy took place. Corruptions are noticed in this century by various writers; Cyprian complains of them in the middle, and Eusebius at the end of it. The latter gives a melancholy account of their change: " that they indulged in luxuries; began to be envious, and quarrelsome, and to dissemble, and falsify their words." That such as these should be found in the army, is not to be marvelled at.

But the professors of christianity were still more degenerate in the fourth century. Lactantius, in his " death of the persecuted," says, " there were christians who assisted at some of the heathen sacrifices. Abundance of evils sprung up in the church in this century. Constantine the Emperor professing to embrace the christian religion, it became the religion of the state : but he introduced into the church, many pagan ceremonies and superstitions, to its great detriment. And what else could be expected, when he did not dispense with the blasphemous titles that had been given to his predecessors of Eternity, Divinity, and Pontifex Maximus. But the christians, pleased with having an Emperor of their own persuasion, submitted to his idolatrous customs, opinions, and innovations upon their religion, sacrificing their consciences to their ease and safety. Thus their scruples against war relaxed, and the unlawfulness of it was given up." And no marvel if it was, when such a mixture of christianity and paganism had taken place in the church.

Now, seeing that the early christians, who lived in the time immediately following that of the apostles, uniformly refused to fight, even in national contests ; and those of the present day plead the lawfulness of war ; how are we to reconcile this contrariety ? My brethren, does it not call for a strict scrutiny, in order to find, from whence came this great change from primitive belief and practice. Let us, with unbiassed minds, examine carefully the connected sense of the doctrine of the New Testament, and let that determine whether or not the horrid practice of slaughtering men under any pretence, can be supported on christian principles.

FINIS.

A

SOLEMN REVIEW

OF THE

CUSTOM OF WAR;

SHOWING

THAT WAR IS THE EFFECT OF POPULAR DELUSON,

AND

PROPOSING A REMEDY.

———

" A glorious success, quietly obtained, is more profitable than the dangers of a battle ; for we ought to esteem those who do what is agreeable to temperance and prudence, no less glorious than those who have gained great reputation by their actions in war." *Vespasian.*

HARTFORD :

....

1815.

SOLEMN REVIEW.

—

SECTION I.

" Shall the sword devour forever ?"

W E regard with horror the custom of the ancient heathens in offering their children in sacrifice to idols. We are shocked with the customs of the Hindoos, in prostrating themselves before the car of an idol to be crushed to death ; in burning women alive on the funeral piles of their husbands ; in offering a monthly sacrifice, by casting living children into the Ganges to be drowned. We read with astonishment of the sacrifices made in the papal crusades, and in the Mahometan and Hindoo pilgrimages. We wonder at the blindness of Christian nations, who have esteemed it right and honorable to buy and sell Africans as property, and reduce them to bondage for life. But that which is fashionable and popular in any country is esteemed right and honorable, whatever may be its nature in the views of men better informed.

But while we look back with a mixture of wonder, indignation and pity, on many of the customs of former ages, are we careful to inquire, whether some customs which we deem honorable, are not the effect of popular delusion ? and whether they will not be so regarded by future generations ? Is it not a fact, that one of the most horrid customs of savage men, is now popular in every nation in Christendom ? What custom of the most barbarous nations is more repugnant to the feelings of piety, humanity and justice, than that of deciding controversies between nations by the edge of the sword, by powder and ball, or the point of the bayonet ? What other savage custom has occasioned half the desolation and misery to the human race ? And what but the grossest infatuation, could render such a custom popular among rational beings ?

When we consider how great a part of mankind have perished by the hands of each other, and how large a portion of human calamity has resulted from war ; it surely cannot appear indifferent, whether this custom is or is not the effect of delusion. Certainly there is no custom which deserves a more thorough examination, than that which has occasioned more slaughter and misery, than all the other abominable customs of the heathen world.

War has been so long fashionable among all nations, that its enormity is but little regarded ; or when thought of at all, it is usually considered as an evil necessary and unavoidable. Perhaps it is really so in the present state of society, and the present views of mankind. But the question to be considered is this ; cannot the state of society and the views of civilized men be so changed as to abolish a barbarous custom, and render wars unnecessary and avoidable ?

If this question may be answered in the affirmative, then we may hope " the sword will not devour forever."

Some may be ready to exclaim, none but God can produce such an effect as the abolition of war ; and we must wait for the millennial day. We admit that God only can produce the necessary change in the state of society, and the views of men ; but God works by human agency and human means. God only could have overthrown the empire of Napoleon ; but this he did by granting success to the efforts of the allied powers. He only could have produced such a change in the views of the British nation, as to abolish the slave trade ; yet the event was brought about by a long course of persevering and honorable exertions of benevolent men.

When the thing was first proposed, it probably appeared to the majority of the people, as an unavailing and chimerical project. But God raised up powerful advocates, gave them the spirit of perseverance, and finally crowned their efforts with glorious success. Now, it is probable, thousands of people are wondering how such an abominable traffic ever had existence in a nation which had the least pretensions to Christianity or civilization. In a similar manner God can put an end to war, and fill the world with astonishment, that rational beings ever thought of such a mode of settling controversies.

As to waiting for the millennium to put an end to war, without any exertions on our own part ; this is like the sinner's waiting God's time for conversion, while he pursues his course of vice and impiety. If ever there shall be a millennium in which the sword will cease to devour, it will probably be effected by the blessing of God on the benevolent exertions of enlightened men. Perhaps no one thing is now a greater obstacle in the way of the wished for state of the church, than the *spirit* and *custom* of war, which is maintained by Christians themselves. Is it not then time, that efforts should be made to enlighten the minds of Christians on a subject of such infinite importance to the happiness of the human race ?

It is not the present object to prove, that a nation may not defend their lives, their liberties and their property against an invading foe ; but to inquire whether it is not possible to effect such a change in the views of men, that there shall be no occasion for *defensive* war. That such a state of things is desirable, no enlightened Christian can deny. That it can be produced without expensive and persevering efforts is not imagined. But are not such efforts to exclude the miseries of war from the world, as laudable as those which have for their object the support of such a malignant and desolating custom ?

The whole amount of property in the United States is probably of far less value, than what has been expended and destroyed within two centuries by wars in Christendom. Suppose, then, that one fifth of this amount had been judiciously laid out by peace associations in the different states and nations, in cultivating the spirit and.art of peace, and in exciting a just abhorrence of war; would not the other four fifths have been in a great measure saved, besides many millions of lives, and an immense portion of misery? Had the whole value of what has been expended in wars, been appropriated to the purpose of peace, how laudable would have been the appropriation, and how blessed the consequences!

SECTION II.

"Shall the sword devour forever?"

That it is possible to produce such a state of society, as to exclude national wars, may appear probable from the following facts.

1. It is impossible for the rulers of any one nation to do much in carrying on a war with another, without the aid of subjects, or the common people.

2. A war between two nations is generally produced by the influence of a small number of ambitious and unprincipled individuals; while the greater part of the nation has no hand in the business until war is proclaimed.

3. A vast majority of every civilized nation, have an aversion to war; such an aversion that it requires much effort and management, to work up their passions so far, that they are willing personally to engage in such hazardous and bloody conflicts. The more any people are civilized and christianized, the greater is their aversion to war; and the more powerful exertions are necessary to excite what is called the war spirit. Were it not for the influence of a few ambitious or revengeful men, an offensive war could not be undertaken with any prospect of success, except when the mass of the people are either uncivilized, or slaves. If then, as great exertions should be made to excite a just abhorrence of war, as have often been made to excite a war spirit, we may be very certain that rulers would find little encouragement to engage in any war, which is not strictly defensive. And as soon as offensive wars shall cease, defensive wars will of course be unknown.

4. It is an affront to common sense, to pretend that military officers and soldiers have no right to inquire whether a war be just or unjust; and that all they have to do is to obey the orders of government. Such a doctrine is fit to be taught only to slaves without souls. If a man is called to fight, he should be faithfully informed, and fully satisfied, that he is not to act the part of a murderer, that the blood of men may not be required at his hands. Every soldier ought to be impressed with the idea, that offensive war is murderous, and that no government on earth has any right to compel him to shed blood in a wanton and aggressive war. Yet in the present state of general delusion, the soldiers and most of the citizens are treated as having no more right to judge of the justice or injustice of a war, than the horses employed in military

service. On one side a war is certainly unjust and murderous. Yet on both sides it is considered as the duty of soldiers to submit to the orders of government, and fight, whether it be murder, or not murder! With the same propriety it might be considered as the duty of a citizen, to obey an order of government for murdering an individual of his own nation.

5. National wars often originate from such petty offences, as would not justify the taking of a single life, and from false principles of honor, which every Christian should abhor. What can be more perfect delusion, than to suppose the *honor* of a nation requires a declaration of war, for such offences as would not justify one individual in taking the life of another? Or what can be more absurd than to suppose the honor of a nation requires going to war, while there is not even the prospect of advantage? Is such petulance, as would disgrace a common citizen, or such a revengeful spirit, as would disgrace a savage, becoming the dignity of a national government, or the ruler of a Christian people?

To sacrifice human beings to false notions of national honor, or to the ambition or avarice of rulers, is no better than to offer them to Moloch, or any other heathen deity. As soon as the eyes of people can be opened to see that war is the effect of delusion, it will then become as unpopular as any other heathenish mode of offering human sacrifices.

It is enough to fill the mind of any reflecting man with horror, to think of the millions of his fellow men who have been sacrificed to the ambition, the avarice, the petulance, or the profligacy of ungodly rulers. How shocking the thought, of armies meeting under the influence of enmity, artificially excited, to plunge their bayonets into the breasts of each other; and thus to offer human sacrifices by thousands, to some idolized phantom of ambitious or revengeful men! In every war that has taken place, the soldiers, on one side or the other, have been either the slaves or the dupes of deluded or unprincipled rulers. The soldiers on each side often meet without ever having experienced the least injury from each other; with no enmity but what has been artificially excited, and without having the least ground to be offended with each other, any more than they had in a time of perfect peace. Yet those who never had any provocation from one another, nor any hand in proclaiming the war, are by art inspired with enmity, and made to thirst for each other's blood, and to perish by each other's hands. A more barbarous mode of offering human sacrifices was never practised by the most savage nations; nor one, it is believed, more abhorrent in the eyes of Heaven.

Public wars and private duels seem to be practised on similar principles. Gentlemen may fight and kill for petty offences; but if common people do the same, they are hanged as murderers. Gentlemen of the sword cannot wait the slow operation of law, for the redress of supposed wrongs, but must show themselves men of spirit, that is, ready to kill for an offensive word. What is deemed honorable virtue in them, is shameful vice in other people. That benevolent, forbearing spirit, which is the glory of good people, is thought beneath the dignity of a gentleman of honor First to give a challenge, and thus notify a man of a wish to kill him, is supposed to exclude the sin of murder. So in regard to war makers, that magnanimity and forbearance, which would adorn the character of a private Christian, is despised by the ambitious ruler in relation to himself. And that petulance, rashness, and disregard to the lives of others, which would render a private citizen the object of just and general abhorrence, are regarded by many, as honorable traits in the character of one who is exalted to rule over men. If in the exercise of this haughty, unfeeling and vindictive temper he declares war, this declaration, he fancies, will secure him from the guilt of murder. Thus thousands after thousands are sacrificed on the altar of his ungodly ambition ; and every means which ingenuity can invent, is employed to delude the unfortunate victims, and make them believe, that with such sacrifices God is well pleased.

There is, however, one circumstance usually attending public wars, which renders them more detestable than private duels. The duellist usually has the generosity to do his own fighting ; but war makers usually have the meanness to avoid the dangers which they create, and to call on other people to fight their battles.

Duelling is indeed a horrible custom ; but war is as much more horrible, as it is more desolating and ruinous. As to the principles on which war is practised, it has no advantage of duelling. It is in fact *national duelling*, attended generally with this dishonorable circumstance, that those who give and accept the challenge, call together a multitude of seconds, and then have not the magnanimity, first to risk their own lives, but they involve their seconds in a bloody contest, while they themselves stand remote from danger, as spectators, or at most as directors of the awful combat. Or perhaps more commonly, after issuing their bloody mandate, they indulge in pleasure, regardless of the suffering of others. So " the king and Haman sat down to drink ; but the city of Shushan was perplexed."

SECTION III.

" Shall the sword devour forever ?"

In favour of war several pleas will probably be made.

First, Some will plead that the Israelites were permitted, and even commanded to make war on the inhabitants of Canaan. To this it may be answered, that the Giver and Arbiter of life had a right, if he pleased, to make use of the savage customs of the age, for punishing guilty nations. If any government of the present day should receive a commission to make war as the Israelites did, let the order be obeyed. But until they have such a commission, let it not be imagined that they can innocently make war.

As a farther answer to this plea, we have to observe, that God has given encouragement, that under the reign of the Messiah, there shall be such a time of peace, " that nation shall not lift up a sword against nation, neither shall they learn war any more." Micah iv. 3. If this prediction shall ever be fulfilled, the present delusion in favor of war must be done away. How then are we to expect the way will be prepared for the accomplishment of the prediction? Probably this is not to be done by miraculous agency, but by the blessing of God on the benevolent exertions of individuals to open the eyes of their fellow mortals, in respect to the evils and delusions of war, and the blessings of peace. Those who shall be the instruments of producing so important a change in the views of men, will be in an eminent sense " peace makers," and will be entitled to the appellation and privileges of " the sons of God." How much more glorious the achievment, to conquer the prejudices and delusions of men on this subject by kindness and reason, than to conquer the world by the edge of the sword!

A second plea in favor of the custom of war may be this—that war is an advantage to a nation, as it usually takes off many vicious and dangerous characters. But does not war make two such characters for every one it removes? Is it not in fact the greatest school of depravity, and the greatest source of mischievous and dangerous characters that ever existed among men? Does not a state of war lower down the standard of morality in a nation, so that a vast portion of common vice is scarcely observed as evil? Let any one who was old enough to observe the state of morals prior to our revolution, ask himself, what was the effect of that war on the morals of New England?

Besides, is it not awful to think of sending vicious men beyond the means of reformation, and the hope of repentance! When they are sent into the army, what is this but consigning them to a state where they will rapidly fill up the measure of their iniquity, and become " fitted to destruction!"

Thirdly, It will be pleaded, that no substitute for war can be devised, which will insure to a nation a redress of wrongs. In reply we may ask, Is it common for a nation to obtain a *redress* of wrongs by war? As to *redress*, do not the wars of nations resemble boxing at a tavern, when both the combatants receive a terrible bruising, then drink a mug of flip together and make peace; each however, bearing for a long time the marks of his folly and madness? A redress of wrongs by war is so uncommon, that unless revenge is redress, and multiplied injuries satisfaction, we should suppose that none but madmen would run the hazard.

But if the eyes of people could be opened in regard to the evils and delusions of war, would it not be easy to form a confederacy of nations, and organize a high court of equity, to decide national controversies? Why might not such a court be composed of some of the most eminent characters from each nation; and a compliance with the decision of the court be made a point of national honor, to prevent the effusion of blood, and to preserve the blessings of peace? Can any considerate person say, that the probability of obtaining right in such a court, would be *less* than by an appeal to arms? When an individual appeals to a court of justice for the redress of wrongs, it is not always the case that he obtains his right. Still such an appeal is more honorable, more safe, and more certain, as well as more benevolent, than for the individual to attempt to obtain a redress by his pis-

tol or his sword. And are not the reasons for avoiding an appeal to
the sword, for the redress of wrongs, always great in proportion to the
calamities, which such an appeal must naturally involve ?   If this be
a fact, then there is infinitely greater reason, why two nations should
avoid an appeal to arms, than usually exists against a bloody combat
between two contending individuals.

In the fourth place it may be urged, that a spirit of forbearance on
the part of a national government, would operate as an invitation to
repeated insult and aggression.

But is this plea founded on facts and experience ?   Does it accord
with what is well known of human nature ?   Who are the persons in
society that most frequently receive insult and abuse ?   Are they the
meek, the benevolent, and the forbearing ?   Do these more commonly
have reason to complain, than persons of quick resentment, who are
ready to fight on the least provocation ?

There are two sects of professed Christians in this country, which,
as sects, are peculiar in their opinions respecting the lawfulness of war,
and the right of repelling injury by violence.   These are the Quakers
and the Shakers.   They are remarkably pacific.   Now we ask, does
it appear from experience that their forbearing spirit, brings on them
a greater portion of injury and insult than what is experienced by
people of other sects ?   Is not the reverse of this true in fact ?   There
may indeed be some instances of such gross depravity, as a person's
taking advantage of their pacific character, to do them injury, with
the hope of impunity.   But in general, it is believed, their pacific
principles and spirit, command the esteem even of the vicious, and
operate as a shield from insult and abuse.

The question may be brought home to every society.   How seldom
do children of a mild, forbearing temper experience insult or injury,
compared with the waspish, who will sting if touched ?   The same
inquiry may be made in respect to persons of these opposite descrip-
tions of every age, and in every situation of life ; and the result will
be favorable to the point in question.

Should any deny the applicability of these examples to national rulers, we have the pleasure of being able to produce one example,
which is undeniably applicable.

When William Penn took the government of Pennsylvania, he distinctly avowed to the Indians his forbearing and pacific principles, and
his benevolent wishes for uninterrupted peace with them.   On these
principles the government was administered, while it remained in the
hands of the Quakers.   What then was the effect ?   Did this pacific
character in government invite aggression and insult ?   Let the answer
be given in the language of the Edinburgh Review of the Life of William Penn.   Speaking of the treaty made by Penn with the Indians,
the Reviewer says :

   " Such indeed was the spirit in which the negotiation was entered
into, and the corresponding settlement conducted, that for the space of
more than *seventy years*—and so long indeed as the Quakers retained
the chief power in the government, the peace and amity which had
been thus solemnly promised and concluded, never was violated ; and

a large though solitary example afforded, of the facility with which they, who are really sincere and friendly in their views, may live in harmony with those who are supposed to be peculiarly fierce and faithless."

Shall then this " solitary" but successful " example" never be imitated ?   " Shall the sword devour forever ?"

SECTION IV.

Some of the evils of war have already been mentioned, but the field is almost boundless.   The demoralizing and depraving effects of war cannot be too seriously considered. We have heard much of the corrupting tendency of some of the rites and customs of the heathen ; but what custom of the heathen nations had a greater effect in depraving the human character than the custom of war ? What is that feeling usually called a *war spirit*, but a deleterious compound of enthusiastic ardor, ambition, malignity and revenge ? a compound which as really endangers the *soul* of the possessor, as the *life* of his enemy ! Who, but a person deranged or deluded, would think it safe to rush into the presence of his Judge with his heart boiling with enmity, and his brothers blood dripping from his hands ? Yet in time of war, how much pains is taken to excite and maintain this blood-thirsty disposition, as essential to success !

The profession of a soldier exposes him to sudden and untimely death, and at the same time hardens his heart, and renders him regardless of his final account.   When a person goes into the army, it is expected of him, that he will rise above the fear of death. In doing this he too commonly rises above the fear of God, and all serious concern for his soul.   It is not denied that some men sustain virtuous characters amidst the contaminating vapors of a camp ; and some may be reformed by a sense of the dangers to which they are exposed ; but these are uncommon occurrences.

The depravity occasioned by war, is not confined to the army. Every species of vice gains ground in a nation during a war.   And when a war is brought to a close, seldom, perhaps, does a community return to its former standard of morals. In time of peace, vice and irreligion generally retain the ground they acquired by war.   As every war augments the amount of national depravity, so it proportionably increases the dangers and miseries of society.*

* *It has been suggested by a friend that there is an exception to this account—that Great Britain has been engaged in war the greater part of the time for a century, and that probably the moral and religious character of the nation has been improved during that period.*

Admitting the correctness of this statement, it amounts to no more than one exception from a general rule ; and this one may be accounted for, on the ground of singular facts.

1. The Island of Great Britain has not been the seat of war for a long course of years.   The wars of that nation have been carried on abroad ; and their army and navy have had little intercourse with the

Among the evil effects of war, a wanton undervaluing of human life ought to be mentioned. This effect may appear in various forms. When a war is declared for the redress of some wrong, in regard to property, if nothing but property be taken into consideration, the result is not commonly better, than spending five hundred dollars in a law suit, to recover a debt of ten. But when we come to estimate human lives against dollars and cents, how are we confounded ! " All that a man hath will he give for his life." Yet, by the custom of war men are so deluded, that a ruler may give fifty or a hundred thousand lives, when only a trifling amount of property is in question, and when the probabilities are as ten to one against him, that even that small amount will not be secured by the contest. It must however again be remarked, that war makers do not usually give their *own lives*, but the *lives of others*. How often has a war been declared with the prospect that not less than 50,000 lives must be sacrificed ; and while the chief agent in making the war would not have given his own life, to secure to his nation every thing that he claimed from the other ? And are rulers to be upheld in thus gambling away the lives of others, while they are careful to secure their own ! If people in general could obtain just views of this species of gambling, rulers would not make offensive wars with impunity. How little do they consider the misery and wretchedness which they bring on those, for whom they should exercise the kindness and care of a father ! Does it not appear that they regard the lives of soldiers as mere property, which they may sacrifice, or barter away at pleasure ? War is in truth the most dreadful species of gambling. Rulers are the gamblers. The lives and property of their subjects are the things they put to hazard in the game ; and be that is most successful in doing mischief, is considered as the best gamester.

If by the custom of war rulers learn to undervalue the lives of their own subjects, how much more do they undervalue the lives of their enemies ! As they learn to hear of the loss of five hundred, or a thousand of their own men, with perhaps less feeling than they would bear of the death of a favorite horse or dog ; so they learn to hear of

population at home. This mode of warfare has tended to remove from their own country the corrupting influence of military camps. Had their Island been the seat of war for eighty years out of a hundred, the effects would, in a great measure, have been reversed. But

2. There have been within 20 years, singular efforts in that nation, which have had a tendency to counteract the moral influence of war. Their Missionary Societies, their Bible Societies, and a vast number of religious, moral, and charitable institutions, must have had a powerful and favorable influence on the character of the nation. By these, and not by wars, the moral state of the nation has been improved.

After all, we are perhaps not very adequate judges of the present depravity in that nation. Their army and navy may still be considered in estimating the amount of national depravity, as well as of population. Let these return home, be disbanded, and mixed with the general mass of citizens ; what then would be the moral state of society in Great Britain ?

the death of thousands after thousands on the side of the enemy, with joy and exultation. If their own men have succeeded in taking an unimportant fortrest, or a frigate, with the loss of fifty lives on their own side, and fifty-one on the other, this is a matter of joy and triumph. This time they have got the game. But alas! at what expense to others! This expense, however, does not interrupt the joy of war makers. They leave it to the wounded and the friends of the dead to *feel* and to *mourn*.

This dreadful depravity of feeling is not confined to rulers in time of war. The army becomes abandoned to such depravity. They learn to undervalue not only the lives of their enemies, but even their own ; and will often wantonly rush into the arms of death, for the sake of military glory. And more or less of the same want of feeling and the same undervaluing of human life, extends through the nation in proportion to the frequency of battles, and the duration of war.

If any thing be done by the army of one nation, which is deemed by the other as contrary to the modern usages in war ; how soon do we hear the exclamations, of *Goths and Vandals !* Yet what are Christians at war, better than those barbarous tribes ? and what is the war spirit in them, better than the spirit of Goths and Vandals ? When the war spirit is excited, it is not always to be circumscribed in its operations, by the refinements of civilization. It is at best a bloody and desolating spirit.

What is our boast of civilization, or christianization, while we tolerate as popular and justifiable the most horrid custom which ever resulted from human wickedness. Should a period arrive when the nations " shall learn war no more ;" what will posterity think of our claims, as Christians and civilized men ? The custom of sacrificing men by war, may appear to them as the *blackest* of all heathen superstitions. Its present popularity may appear as wonderful to ages to come, as the past popularity of any ancient custom now does to us. What ! they may exclaim, could those be *Christians*, who would sacrifice men by thousands to a point of *honor*, falsely so called ; or to obtain a redress of a trifling wrong in regard to property ! If such were the customs of Christians, what were they better than the heathens of their own time ?

Perhaps some apologist may rise up in that day, and plead, that it appears from the history of our times, that it was supposed necessary to the safety of a nation, that its government should be quick to assume a warlike tone and attitude, upon every infringement of their rights ; that magnanimous forbearance was considered as pusillanimity, and that Christian meekness was thought intolerable in the character of a ruler.

To this others may reply—Could these professed Christians imagine, that their safety depended on displaying a spirit the reverse of their Master's ? Could they suppose such a temper best calculated to insure the protection of Him, who held their destiny in his hands ? Did they not know that wars were of a demoralizing tendency, and that the greatest danger of a nation resulted from its corruption and depravity ? Did they not also know, that a haughty spirit of resentment in one government, was very sure to provoke a similar spirit in another? that one war usually paved the way for a repetition of similar calamities, by depraving each of the contending parties, and by fixing enmities and jealousies, which would be ready to break forth on the most frivolous occasions?

SECTION V.

That we may obtain a still clearer view of the delusions of war, let us look back to the origin of society. Suppose a family, like that of Noah, to commence the settlement of a country. They multiply into a number of distinct families. Then in the course of years they become so numerous as to form distinct governments. In any stage of their progress, unfortunate disputes might arise by the imprudence, the avarice, or the ambition of individuals.

Now at what period would it be proper to introduce the custom of deciding controversies by the edge of the sword, or an appeal to arms? Might this be done when the families had increased to ten? Who would not be shocked at the madness of introducing such a custom under such circumstances? Might it then with more propriety be done when the families had multiplied to fifty, or to a hundred, or a thousand, or ten thousand? The greater the number, the greater the danger, the greater the carnage and calamity. Besides, what reason can be given, why this mode of deciding controversies would not be as proper when there were but ten families, as when there were ten thousand. And why might not two individuals thus decide disputes, as well as two nations?

Perhaps all will admit that the custom could not be honorably introduced, until they separated, and formed two or more distinct governments. But would this change of circumstances dissolve their ties as brethren, and their obligations as accountable beings? Would the organization of distinct governments confer a right on rulers to appeal to arms for the settlement of controversies? Is it not manifest, that no period can be assigned, at which the introduction of such a custom would not be absolute murder? And shall a custom which must have been murderous at its commencement, be now upheld as necessary and honorable!

But, says the objector, in determining the question, whether war is now the effect of delusion, we must consider what mankind *are*, and not what they would have been, had wars never been introduced.

To this we reply: We should consider both; and by what *ought* to have been the state of society, we may discover the present delusion, and the need of light and reformation. If it would have been to the honor of the human race, had the custom of war never commenced, it must be desirable to dispel the present darkness, and exterminate the desolating scourge The same objection might have been made to the proposition in the British Parliament for the abolition of the slave trade: the same may now be made against any attempt to abolish the custom of human sacrifices among the Hindoos; yea, the same may be urged against every attempt to root out pernicious and immoral customs of long standing.

Let it then be seriouly considered, how abominably murderous the custom must have been in its origin ; how precarious the mode of obtaining redress ; how often the aggressor is successful ; how small a part even of the successful nation is ever benefitted by the war ; how a nation is almost uniformly impoverished by the contest ; how many individuals are absolutely ruined as to property, or morals, or both ; and what a multitude of fellow creatures are hurried into eternity in an untimely manner, and an unprepared state. And who can hesitate a moment to denounce war as the effect of popular delusion ?

Let every Christian seriously consider the malignant nature of that spirit, which war makers evidently wish to excite, and compare it with the temper of Jesus, and where is the Christian who would not shudder at the thought of dying in the exercise of the common war spirit, and also at the thought of being the instrument of exciting such a spirit in his fellow men ? Any custom which cannot be supported but by exciting in men the very temper of the devil, ought surely to be banished from the Christian world.

The impression, that aggressive war is murderous, is general among Christians, if not universal. The justness of this impression seems to be admitted by almost every government in going to war. For this reason each of two governments endeavors to fix on the other the charge of aggression, and to assume to itself the ground of defending some right, or avenging some wrong. Thus each excuses itself, and charges the other with all the blood and misery, which results from the contest.

These facts, however, are so far from affording a plea in favor of the custom of war, that they afford a weighty reason for its abolition. If in the view of conscience, the aggressor is a murderer, and answerable for the blood shed in war ; if one or the other must be viewed by God as the aggressor ; and if such is the delusion attending war, that each party is liable to consider the other as the aggressor ; surely there must be serious danger of a nation's being involved in the guilt of murder, while they imagine they have a cause which may be justified.

So prone are men to be blinded by their passions, their prejudices and their interests, that in most private quarrels, each of two individuals persuades himself that he is in the right, and his neighbour in the wrong. Hence the propriety of arbitrations, references, and appeals to courts of justice, that persons more disinterested may judge, and prevent that injustice and desolation, which would result from deciding private disputes by single combat or acts of violence.

But rulers of nations are as liable to be misled by their passions and interests as other men ; and when misled, they are very sure to mislead those of their subjects, who have confidence in their wisdom and integrity. Hence it is highly important that the custom of war should be abolished, and some other mode adopted, to settle disputes between nations. In private disputes there may be cause of complaint on each side, while neither has reason to shed the blood of the other ; much less to shed the blood of innocent family connexions, neighbours and friends. So of two nations, each may have cause of complaint, while neither can be justified in making war; and much less in shedding the blood of innocent people, who have had no hand in giving the offence.

It is an awful feature in the character of war, and a strong reason why it should not be countenanced, that it involves the innocent with the guilty in the calamities it inflicts ; and often falls with the greatest vengeance on those who have had no concern in the management of national affairs. It surely is not a crime to be born in a country, which is afterwards invaded ; yet in how many instances do war makers punish or destroy, for no other crime, than being a native or resident of an invaded territory. A mode of revenge or redress, which makes no distinction between the innocent and the guilty, ought to be discountenanced by every friend to justice and humanity.

Besides, as the rulers of a nation are as liable as other people, to be governed by passion and prejudice, there is as little prospect of justice in permitting war for the decision of national disputes, as there would be in permitting an incensed individual to be, in his own cause complainant, witness, judge, jury and executioner. In what point of view, then, is war not to be regarded with horror ?

SECTION VI.

" Shall the sword devour forever ?"

That wars have been so over-ruled by God, as to be the occasion of some benefits to mankind, will not be denied; for the same may be said of every fashion or custom that ever was popular among men. War may have been the occasion of advancing useful arts and sciences, and even of the spread of the gospel. But we are not to do evil that good may come, nor to countenance evil because God may over-rule it for good.

One advantage of war, which has often been mentioned, is this— it gives opportunity for the display of extraordinary talents, of daring enterprize and intrepidity. But let robbery and piracy become as popular as war has been, and will not these customs give as great opportunity for the display of the same talents and qualities of mind? Shall we therefore encourage robbery and piracy ? Indeed it may be asked, do we not encourage these crimes ? For what is modern warfare but a popular, refined and legalized mode of robbery, piracy, and murder, preceded by a proclamation, giving notice of the purpose of the war maker ? But whether such a proclamation changes the character of the following enormities, is a question to be decided at a higher court than that of any earthly sovereign, and by a law superior to the law of nations.

The answer of a pirate to Alexander the Great, was as just as it was severe : " By what right," said the king, " do you infest the seas ?" The pirate replied, " By the same that you infest the universe. But because I do it in a small ship, I am called a robber ; and because you do the same acts with a great fleet, you are called a conqueror."

Equally just was the language of the Scythian ambassadors to the same deluded monarch : " Thou boastest, that the only design of thy marches is to extirpate robbers. *Thou thyself art the greatest robber in the world.*"

May we then plead for the custom of war, because it produces such mighty robbers as Alexander ? Or if once in an age it should produce such a character as Washington, will this make amends for the slaughter of twenty millions of human beings, and all the other concomitant evils of war !

If the characters of such men as Alexander had been held in just abhorrence by mankind, this single circumstance would probably have saved many millions from untimely death. But the celebrity which delusion has given to that desolating robber, and the renown attached to his splendid crimes, have excited the ambition of others, in every succeeding age, and filled the world with misery and blood.

Is it not then time for Christians to learn *not* to attach glory to guilt, or to praise actions which God will condemn ? That Alexander possessed talents worthy of admiration, will be admitted. But when such talents are prostituted to the vile purpose of military fame, by spreading destruction and misery through the world, a character is formed, which should be branded with everlasting infamy. And nothing perhaps short of the commission of such atrocious deeds, can more endanger the welfare of community, than the applause given to successful military desperadoes. Murder and robbery are not the less criminal for being perpetrated by a king, or a mighty warrior. Nor will the applause of deluded mortals secure such monsters from the vengeance of Heaven.

Dr. Prideaux states, that in fifty battles fought by Cæsar, he slew *one million, one hundred and ninety-two thousand* of his enemies. If to this number we add the loss of troops on his own side, and the slaughter of women and children on both sides, we shall probably have a total of TWO MILLIONS of human beings, sacrificed to the ambition of one man.

If we assign an equal number to Alexander, and the same to Napoleon, which we probably may do with justice, then to *three* military butchers, we may ascribe the untimely death of SIX MILLIONS of the human family : A number equal to the whole population of the United States, in the year 1800. Is it not then reasonable to believe that a greater number of human beings have been slain by the murderous custom of war, than the whole amount of the present population of the world ? To what heathen deity was there ever offered such a multitude of human sacrifices, as have been offered to human ambition ?

Shall then the Christian world remain silent in regard to the enormity of this custom, and even applaud the deeds of men, who were a *curse* to the age in which they lived ? men whose talents were employed, not in advancing the happiness of the human race, but in spreading desolation and misery through the world ! On the same principle that such men are applauded, we may applaud the chief of a band of robbers and pirates in proportion to his ingenuity, intrepidity, and address, in doing mischief. If the chief displays these energies of mind in a high degree in a successful course of plundering and murder, then he is a " *mighty hunter*," a man of great renown.

But if we attach glory to such exploits, do we not encourage others to adopt the same road to fame ? Besides, would not such applause betray a most depraved taste ; a taste which makes no proper distinction between virtue and vice, or doing good and doing mischief ; a taste to be captivated with the glare of bold exploits, but regardless of the *end* to which they were directed, the *means* by which they were accomplished, the *misery* which they occasioned to others, and the light in which they must be viewed by a benevolent God ?

SECTION VII.

An important question now occurs. By what means is it possible to produce such a change in the state of society, and the views of Christian nations, that every ruler shall feel that his own honor, safety and happiness, depend on his displaying a pacific spirit, and forbearing to engage in offensive wars ? Is it not possible to form powerful peace societies, in every nation of Christendom, whose object shall be, to support government and secure the nation from war ?

In such societies we may hope to engage every true minister of the Prince of Peace, and every Christian who possesses the temper of his Master. In this number would be included a large portion of important civil characters.

Having formed societies for this purpose, let the contributions be liberal, in some measure corresponding with the magnitude and importance of the object. Let these be judiciously appropriated to the purpose of diffusing light, and the spirit of peace in every direction, and for exciting a just abhorrence of war in every breast.

Let printing presses be established in sufficient numbers to fill every land with news papers, tracts and periodical works, adapted to the pacific design of the societies. Let these all be calculated for the support and encouragement of good rulers, and for the cultivation of a mild and pacific temper among every class of citizens.

The object would be so perfectly harmonious with the spirit, the design, and the glory of the gospel, that it might be frequently the subject of discussion in the pulpit ; the subject of Sabbath and every day conversation, and be introduced into our daily prayers to God, whether in public or private.

Another means of advancing the object, deserves particular consideration ; namely, early education. This grand object should have a place in every plan of education, in families, common schools, academies and universities.

" Train up a child in the way he should go, and when he is old, he will not depart from it." The power of education has been tried, to make children of a ferocious, blood-thirsty character. Let it now have a fair chance, to see what it will do towards making mild, friendly and peaceful citizens.

As there is an aversion to war in the breast of a large majority of people in every civilized community; and as its evils have been recently felt in every Christian nation; is there not ground to hope, that it would be as easy to excite a disposition for peace, as a disposition for war? If then, peace societies should be formed, and such means be put in operation, as have been suggested, is it not very certain, that the most beneficial effects would result? Would they not gradually produce an important change in the views and state of society, and give a new character to Christian nations? What institution or project would more naturally unite all pious and virtuous men? And on what efforts could we more reasonably hope for the blessing of the God of peace?

Should prudent, vigorous, and well conducted efforts be made, in a century from this time, the nations of Christendom may consider human sacrifices, made by war, in the same light they now view the ancient sacrifices to Moloch; or in the light of wanton and deliberate murder. And such a change in the views of men must conduce to the security and stability of human governments, and to the felicity of the world. As soon as Christian nations are impressed with the importance of this change, they may find access to the heathen. But while Christians indulge the custom of war, which is in truth the very worst custom in the world, with what face can they reprove the heathen, or assume among them the office of instructers! "Physician, heal thyself."

The Bible Societies, already formed in various parts of the world, must naturally, and even necessarily aid the object now proposed. Indeed, the two objects are so congenial, that whatever promotes the one, will aid the other. Nor is it easy to see how any Bible Society could refrain from voluntarily affording all possible encouragement to peace societies. The same may be said of all missionary societies, and societies for propagating the gospel. Should these all cordially co-operate, they must form a most powerful association.

But our hopes and expectations are not limited here. The societies of Friends and Shakers will come in of course, and cordially contribute to the glorious object. May we not also expect a ready acquiescence from the particular churches of every denomination in the land? And why may we not look to the various literary and political societies, for aid in a plan which has the security, the peace, and the happiness of the world for its object.

That there are obstacles and objections to be encountered we cannot deny; but it is confidently believed, that there are none insurmountable; because God will aid in such a cause, and the time is at hand, when his prediction shall be fulfilled.

As the object is not of a party nature, and as party distinctions, and party purposes have been excluded from the discussion, it is hoped no objection will arise from the present state of political parties in this country. The supposed delusion in respect to war, is confined to no nation, nor to any political sect in any country. What has been said on the subject has not been designed for the purpose of reproach against any class of men; but with a desire to befriend and benefit all who have not examined the subject ; and to rouse Christians to one united and vigorous effort to bless the world with peace.

An eloquent speech delivered by Mr. Wilberforce in the British Parliament, in favor of propagating Christianity in India, with a view to abolish human sacrifices in that country, contains some observations, which we hope he will repeat in the same house on the present subject :

"It was," said he, "formerly my task to plead the cause of a people whose woes affected every heart, and who were finally rescued from the situation in which they groaned, by the abolition of the slave trade. That cause was doubtless the cause of suffering humanity ; but I declare, that if we entirely exclude the consideration of religion, humanity appears to me to be still more concerned in the cause I am now pleading, than in that for which I was formerly the advocate."—— "I, for my part, consider it as absolute blasphemy to believe that that great Being, to whom we owe our existence, has doomed so large a portion of mankind to remain forever in that state in which we see the natives of India at this day. I am confident his Providence has furnished remedies fitted to the case, and I hold it to be our duty to apply them. And I am satisfied, that not only may this be safely attempted, but that its accomplishment will be in the highest degree beneficial.

May God grant that this powerful advocate for "suffering humanity" may have his heart fervently engaged for the abolition of the *war trade*. Here he may find a new and ample field for the display of his piety, his philanthropy and his eloquence. With the greatest propriety he may state, that the miseries occasioned by the universal custom of war, are far more dreadful, than those occasioned by either of the limited customs, for the abolition of which he has so honorably and successfully contended.

If it would be blasphemy to believe that God has doomed so great a portion of his creatures as the natives of India, to remain forever the subjects of their present delusions respecting human sacrifices ; can it be less than blasphemy to believe that he has doomed not only all Christendom, but all the nations of the earth, to be forever so deluded, as to support the most desolating custom which ever resulted from human depravity, or which ever afflicted the race of Adam ? Here with sincerity I can adopt the words of Mr. Wilberforce—"I am confident that his providence has furnished remedies fitted to the case ; and I hold it to be our duty to apply them."

I have till now avoided the mention of our present war, that nothing should appear calculated to excite party feelings. But as the present calamity is severely felt, I must be permitted to express my hope, that the affliction will favor the present object. If our distresses may be the occasion of opening the eyes of this people to see the delusions of war in general, and of exciting them to suitable exertions to prevent a return of such a calamity, an important benefit may result not only to posterity, but to the world. For if suitable exertions should be made in this country, the influence will not be bounded by the Atlantic ; it will cross the ocean, and find its way into the Bible

Societies, and other religious societies in Great Britain, and on the continents of Europe, Asia and Africa. Nor will it be many years before it will find access to the Houses of legislation and the Palaces of kings.

Here Christians of every sect may find an object worthy of their attention, and in which they may cordially unite. For this object they may with propriety leave behind all party zeal and party distinctions, and bury their animosities in one united effort, to give peace to the world.

Let lawyers, politicians and divines, and men of every class who can write or speak, consecrate their talents to the diffusion of light, and love, and peace. Should there be an effort, such as the object demands, God will grant his blessing, posterity will be grateful, heaven will be filled with joy and praise, and " the sword shall *not* devour forever."

SECTION VIII.

Let not the universality of the custom be regarded as an objection to making the attempt. If the custom be wicked and destructive, the more universal, the more important is a reformation. If war is ever to be set aside, an effort must some time be made ; and why not now as well as at any future day ? What objection can now be stated, which may not be brought forward at any after period ?

If men must have objects for the display of heroism, let their intrepidity be shown in firmly meeting the formidable prejudices of a world in favor of war. Here is an opportunity for the display of such heroism as will occasion no remorse on a dying bed, and such as God will approve at the final reckoning. In this cause, ardent zeal, genuine patriotism, undaunted fortitude, the spirit of enterprize, and every quality of mind worthy of a hero, may be gloriously displayed. Who ever displayed a more heroic spirit than Saint Paul ? For such heroism and love of country as he displayed, the object now proposed will open the most ample field at home and abroad.

That there is nothing in the nature of mankind, which renders war necessary and unavoidable—nothing which inclines them to it which may not be overcome by the power of education, may appear from what is discoverable in the two sects already mentioned. The Quakers and Shakers are of the same nature with other people, " men of like passions" with those who uphold the custom of war. All the difference between them and others results from education and habit. The principles of their teachers are diffused through their societies, impressed on the minds of old and young ; and an aversion to war and violence is excited, which becomes habitual, and has a governing influence on their hearts, their passions and their lives.

If then it has been proved to be *possible*, by the force of education, to produce such an aversion to war, that people will not even *defend* their own lives by acts of violence ; shall it be thought impossible by similar means, to destroy the popularity of *offensive* war, and exclude the deadly custom from the abodes of men ?

The following things will perhaps be generally admitted ; that the Christian religion has abolished the practice of enslaving captives, and in several respects mitigated the evils of war, by introducing milder usages ; that if the temper of our Saviour should universally prevail among men, wars *must cease* to the ends of the earth ; that the scriptures give reason to hope such a time of peace will result from the influence of the Christian religion.

If these views and expectations are well founded, does it not follow of course, that the spirit and custom of war is directly opposed to the principles and spirit of the gospel ; that in proportion as the gospel has its proper effect on the minds of men, an aversion to war must be excited ; and that it is the duty of every Christian to do all in his power to bring the custom into disrepute, and to effect its abolition ?

Can it be consistent with due regard to the gospel, for Christians to hold their peace, while they see a custom prevailing, which annually sweeps off myriads of their brethren, hurrying them into eternity by violence and murder ? Can they forbear to exert themselves, to put an end to this *voluntary plague ?* Can we feel a conviction that war is in its nature opposed to the principles and spirit of our religion, and that it is the purpose of God to put an end to this scourge by the influence of the gospel ; and still sleep on without any effort to produce the effect which we believe is intended by our heavenly Father ?

If the Christian religion is to put an end to war, it must be by the efforts of those who are under its influence. So long therefore as Christians acquiesce in the custom, the desirable event will be delayed.

Christianity is not itself a powerful intelligent *agent*. It is neither a God, an angel, nor a man. It is only a system of divine instructions, relating to *duty* and *happiness ;* to be used by men for their own benefit, the benefit of each other, and the honor of its Author. Like all other instructions, they are of no use any farther than they are regarded and reduced to practice.

In what way then is it possible that Christianity should put an end to war, but by enlightening the minds of men, as to the evil of the custom, and exciting them to an opposite course of conduct ? Is it *possible* that the custom of war should be abolished by the influence of religion, while Christians themselves are its advocates ?

If God has appointed that men shall be saved by the *preaching* of the gospel, the gospel *must be preached*, or the *end* will never be accomplished. So if he has appointed that by the same gospel this world shall be delived from war, this also must be effected by similar means. The tendency of the gospel to this effect must be illustrated and enforced ; its opposition to war must be displayed in the *lives of Christians ;* and men must be influenced by gospel motives to cease from destroying one another.

There are other effects which we expect will be produced by Christianity, namely, the abolition of *heathen idolatry*, and the various modes of offering *human sacrifices*. But how are these events to be

brought about? Do we expect that our Bibles will spread their covers
for wings, fly through the world, and convert the nations without the
agency of Christians? Should we expect the gospel would ever convert the heathen from their idolatry, if those who profess to be its
friends, should themselves generally encourage idolaters in their present
courses, by a compliance with their customs? Such expectations would
be just as reasonable, as to expect the gospel will occasion wars to cease,
without the exertions of Christians, and while they countenance the
custom by their own examples.

It will perhaps be pleaded that mankind are not yet sufficiently enlightened, to apply the principles of the gospel for the abolition of
war; and that we must wait for a more improved state of society.
Improved in what? in the science of blood? Are such improvements
to prepare the way for peace? Why not wait a few centuries, until
the natives of India become more improved in their idolatrous customs,
before we attempt to convert them to Christianity? Do we expect that
by continuing in the practice of idolatry, their minds will be prepared
to receive the gospel? If not, let us be consistent, and while we use
means for the conversion of heathens, let means also be used for the
conversion of Christians. For war is in fact a heathenish and savage
custom, of the most malignant, most desolating, and most horrible
character. It is the greatest curse, and results from the grossest delusions that ever afflicted a guilty world.

NOTE.

*After the preceding pages were chiefly in type, I saw for the first
time "The COMPLAINT OF PEACE" and "ANTIPOLEMUS" written by
Erasmus. The coincidence of opinions and remarks must strike every
reader who shall compare the writings of Erasmus with this Review.
He will, however, also perceive a disparity of eloquence not much to
the honor of the latter. But should the Review be only the occasion of
exciting Christians to read the more important work of Erasmus, my
labor will neither be in vain nor regretted. In his discussion of the
subject, there is a display of reason, religion, and eloquence, calculated
to convince every mind which is not strongly fortified by the delusions of
prejudice, and to interest every heart which is less hardened than Pharaoh's. It is indeed astonishing that even popish prejudices could resist
the force of his reasoning against the custom of war. As a specimen of
his spirit and style, we quote the following passages, in reference to the
custom of using the symbol of the Cross for a standard, partaking of the
Lord's Supper before going to battle, and saying the Lord's Prayer.*

"The absurdest circumstance of all those respecting the use of the
CROSS as a standard is, that you see it glittering and waving high in air,
in both the contending armies at once. Divine service is performed to
the same Christ in both armies at the same time. What a shocking

fight! Lo! Crosses *dashing against* Crosses, *and* Christ *on this side* firing bullets *at* Christ *on the other; Cross against Cross, and Christ against Christ!" He adds :—*

" *Let us now imagine we hear a soldier among these* fighting *Christians sayingt he Lord's prayer.* "Our Father," *says he : O, hardened wretch! can you call* him Father, *when you are just going to cut your* brother's *throat ?* " Hallowed be thy name :" *how can the name of God be more impiously* unhallowed, *than by mutual bloody murder among you, his sons?* " Thy kingdom come :" *do you pray for the coming* of his kingdom, *while you are endeavoring to establish an earthly despotism, by the spilling of the blood of God's sons and subjects ?* " Thy will be done in earth as it is in heaven :" *His will in heaven is for* peace, *but you are now meditating* war. *Dare you say to your father in heaven,* " Give us this day our daily bread," *when you are going the next minute to burn your* brother's cornfields ; *and had rather lose the benefits of them yourself, than suffer him to enjoy them unmolested ? With what face can you say,* " Forgive us our trespasses as we forgive those who trespass against us," *when so far from forgiving your own brother, you are going with all the haste you can, to murder him in cold blood, for an alleged trespass, which after all is but imaginary? Do you presume to deprecate* danger *of* "temptation," *who, not without great danger to yourself, are doing all you can to force your* brother *into danger? Do you deserve to be* delivered from evil, *that is, from the evil being to whose impulse you submit yourself, and by whose spirit you are guided, in contriving the greatest possible evil to your brother ?"*

It may be doubted whether a complete history of all the conduct of infernal spirits, would contain any thing more inconsistent, more abominable, or more to be deplored, than has appeared in the history of warring Christians. *To behold two contending armies, from Christian nations, so deluded as mutually to offer prayers to the same benevolent God, for success in their attempts to butcher each other, is enough to fill the mind of any considerate person with amazement and horror. Yea, a sight like this might cause weeping in heaven, and triumph in hell!*